Balanced Boundaries

Achieving self-improvement, Managing relationships effectively and Overcoming emotional barriers

S.H. Rhodes

Contents

Introduction

Hi, my name is Siou Han, and I would like to tell you the story of how boundaries saved my life.

I know that sounds dramatic, but it's the truth. For so long, I had found myself unhappy and couldn't understand why. On the surface, you'd think my life was going well. I was striving my best to be a good role model to my younger siblings and cousins. I made sure to excel at my studies. I had done a great job at blending into the Western society I had become a part of. I had carried the weight of my family's expectations, trying to make them proud.

It took me a long time to realize the cost of all these things. That, in working so hard to be all these things and do all these things, I was sacrificing parts of myself. Each time I compromised my own happiness for the sake of someone else's, I was giving away another little part of myself.

In the end, I had given away so much that I had nothing left.

The lack of boundaries had led me to a place where I felt burnt out and depleted. I was so unhappy, and I couldn't understand why. Once I had identified the source of all my discomfort, I began the long journey to recovering the parts of myself that I had spent all those years giving away.

Only once I learned how to set boundaries in my life did I slowly begin piecing myself back together again.

So, I'm going to introduce you to these personal protection mechanisms in a way that you've probably never thought of before. People see boundaries as barriers you establish to separate yourself from other people. Thinking of them in this way can make them seem negative or selfish. What they really do, however, is protect you from sacrificing too much of yourself. If you can't see the line between you and other people, you will end up giving away too much of yourself, just like I did.

In my relationships, I found that the lack of boundaries had caused me to resent my family. For so long, I had worked to be the perfect older sibling, a person the others could look up to and want to be like. In doing that, I had to put aside the things I wanted. I had to be the person they needed me to be instead of the person I was. The pressure was unbearable. I felt as though every tiny one of my failures was another way that I had let them down, that if they made the same mistakes, it would be my fault. I had to bear the weight of the consequences of my actions as well as theirs.

Establishing limits to how much I was willing to tolerate taught me to separate myself from others. As much as I needed to set a good example, I also had to stay true to myself. I had to see that each of us is responsible for our own futures and that, as much as I could try and be a great role model, it wasn't up to me whether or not my younger family members chose to follow suit.

When it came to being a foreigner, feeling the need to fit in made me sacrifice so much of my identity. I wanted so badly to blend into a new culture that I ended up letting go of important parts of my own—the things that had made me who I was—and my rich cultural heritage. Learning to take control in this area of my life meant finally giving myself permission to be proud of my background, to see it not as less than or something to be embarrassed of. It meant not hiding parts of my upbringing that were important to me just because I was afraid people wouldn't understand or would judge or mock me. I had to give myself the right to be proud of being an immigrant.

Maybe you find yourself in the same place I was. Maybe you feel like you've compromised too much of yourself for the sake of others, and their expectations are weighing you down. The good news is that you don't need to feel that way anymore! I'm going to share the journey I undertook to free myself from the pressure of other people's expectations and how I learned to follow my own path.

By learning how to set and implement effective boundaries in all areas of your life, you, too, can find the freedom you deserve. Establishing limits can be a potent tool for personal development. When you learn how to set them, you realize how important it is to prioritize your happiness and peace of mind. It's a self-care and self-actualization practice, not a selfish one.

Boundaries protect you from losing yourself. They can help you pursue the things you want without sacrificing your own happiness or feeling guilty. They allow you to adapt to society without disappearing into it. You can have your own identity and still appreciate those of others. You don't need to be ashamed of who you are to fit in, and you don't need to give up the things you enjoy to be a good role model.

Having these measures in place sets the tone for your relationships with others and creates guidelines for how other people should treat you. When you have set boundaries, people learn to respect your limitations and appreciate your efforts. You are not responsible for other people, and it is not your job to be the person they expect you to be. Being everything to everyone will leave you with nothing left to give to yourself.

As we embark on this journey, I will share stories of how defining my needs has improved my life in amazing ways. By reading about how I have learned to embrace who I am and how to put myself first, I hope you can use this book to begin your own journey of transformation. I hope the tools you find here will empower you to begin living your life on the terms you've defined for yourself. Through this process, I hope you learn more about yourself and grow a new understanding of what's important to you and how best to pursue the things that bring you joy.

May this journey fill you with the courage you need to forge your own path and live the life that you deserve. I hope that, in setting boundaries, you will set yourself free.

1. The Fundamentals of Boundaries

Healthy boundaries are not walls. They are the gates and fences that allow you to enjoy the beauty of your own garden.

— Lydia Hall

I used to imagine boundaries as a figurative line in the sand over which people should dare not cross. I saw them as a prison people built around themselves to keep others out. I think those perceptions are why I always found my total openness to be a positive trait. I thought not having boundaries meant I was more selfless. I was the person people knew they could come to when they were in need because they knew I would never turn them away. I thought not having limits made me a kinder, better person.

I clearly didn't understand boundaries at all. It's true when they say that knowledge is power. The more I learned about boundaries, the more I realized how desperately I needed them. It was only once I sat down and started learning about them that I finally understood their purpose and their importance. My assumptions had kept me from the opportunity that expressing my needs would have given me to transform my life much earlier on.

I'm hoping you will come to the same realization over the course of our journey together. In this chapter, I'll try to make this hope a reality by exploring the truth of what boundaries are with you. By the end of it, you will see for yourself why they're such a fundamental aspect of personal growth and development.

Defining Boundaries

Boundaries are the limits you set for yourself that define how you'd like people to treat you. We all have them in one form or another. Like all of us, you have things you like and those that annoy you. Making them known can govern your relationships and interactions with those around you and let them know what you are and are not comfortable with. When you don't communicate your needs with others, they're more likely to overstep them.

On top of this, healthy boundaries allow you to thrive in your dealings with people and form relationships based on mutual respect. You're less likely to be mistreated and taken for granted when others know what lines not to cross with you. When you set personal limits, you give yourself the ability to protect your own mental health and general well-being.

Types of Boundaries

There are six main types of boundaries that govern the different aspects of our lives. Let's discuss them below:

Emotional Boundaries

Emotional boundaries are there to protect your right to have your own thoughts and feelings and to not allow others to try and tell you how to feel or invalidate your reactions. They exist to help you teach people how to treat and speak to you. They also keep you from having to feel responsible for other people's emotions because, remember: You are only responsible for how you feel, not for the thoughts and feelings of others.

When you have emotional boundaries, you can avoid putting yourself in situations that leave you feeling vulnerable and exposed. You also protect yourself from having other people use you as an emotional dumping ground for their problems, and you block them from sharing information with you that's inappropriate for the nature of your relationship.

An example of a good relationship to start learning how to set up emotional boundaries is one where you have a friend who is always coming to you with their problems and expecting you to support them through their struggles. However, they never reciprocate. Putting protective mechanisms in place will protect your peace and your energy from being exploited by other people.

Physical Boundaries

Physical boundaries prevent your personal space from being infringed on by other people. They are the invisible barriers that protect your body from unwanted contact with other people, and they also ensure your privacy. They let people know how close they can get to you and whether or not you're comfortable with being touched and where. They assert your right to fulfill your physical needs, such as eating and sleeping. Physical boundaries remind people that your body and personal space belong to you and only you.

An example of one is if you're waiting in line at a store and the person behind you keeps getting too close to you. You can simply let them know that they're invading your personal space and making you uncomfortable, and you can request that they move a few steps back from you.

Sexual Boundaries

Sexual boundaries are a way to protect your right to consent to intimacy and to what extent in a way that makes you comfortable. Clearly defining this with your partner is a matter of talking to them about what your sexual needs and desires are and also sharing what you aren't comfortable with. They also include your right to refuse unwanted sexual advances and inappropriate comments from others.

When you're starting a new relationship, it's important that you communicate your comfort levels with your partner before any intimacy happens. You both need to walk into any encounters already knowing what the other is comfortable with and what each other's limitations are.

Spiritual Boundaries

Spiritual or religious boundaries protect your right to hold whatever beliefs you choose. They also protect your right to express those beliefs in whichever way you feel comfortable with, be it in the way you choose to worship or the way you practice your faith. For example, if you want to say a prayer before you eat, you're allowed to do that even if the people you're with choose not to.

Material and Financial Boundaries

Material and financial boundaries protect your finances and belongings from being misused by other people. You have a right to spend your money how you want and are under no obligation to purchase things for others or to loan them money. People should also respect your possessions and not take or use them without your prior consent. Financial boundaries also safeguard your right to be fairly remunerated by your employer.

An example of a material boundary is if you have a roommate who is constantly wearing your clothes or using your stuff without your permission, especially when these items are stored in a non-communal area. They might assume it's alright with you since you share a living space and are friends, but you need to express to them that they have to respect you by asking before making use of your things.

Time Boundaries

Time is a resource that boundaries guard, both how much of it you have and how you choose to spend it. You are under no obligation to use your time on people or activities that you don't want to. Others also have no right to waste your time or expect you to sacrifice it for them without compensating you in some way.

A good example would be if you set up coffee dates with a friend, and they're consistently late for them. Putting up a boundary with them would mean letting them know that, if they don't value your time, you're not going to continue giving them any of it.

The Role of Boundaries in Personal and Professional Life

Setting boundaries in your personal and professional life will keep you from feeling overextended in both areas. Without clear lines separating them, they will begin to overlap with each other. As a consequence, you'll feel drained, and it may lead to burnout.

Perhaps mine is a story you can relate to.

As far as my personal relationships were concerned, I used to think that it made me a great friend to be available to everyone's every need. I would tell my friends that they could always count on me when they needed me, no matter what time of day it was. On the surface, this is a very noble and selfless promise, but, in reality, it's not. You can't possibly make yourself available to people 24/7 and trying to be can lead to people taking advantage of your kindness, and trust me, they will!

When it came to my professional life, I was the same. I was always the employee who would stay for hours after the day had ended to finish a project on time. I would take work home with me and focus on it well into the night in order to meet a deadline. Again, on the surface, this might appear admirable, and my employers often praised my work ethic. But it was extremely unhealthy to live this way, and I soon realized that my job had overtaken my life to a point where everything else had almost ceased to exist.

The most important thing to note in all of this selfless sacrifice is that it left me no time to myself. I was so busy being the most available friend and the most hardworking employee that I had completely neglected myself. I never found the time to do the things I enjoyed or have evenings to unwind and relax. There was always something else or someone else taking up all of my energy.

So, learning from my example of not having these safeguards, let's talk about why having boundaries in your work and professional life is important and how they will help boost both of these aspects.

Personal Boundaries

Having personal boundaries will maintain mutual understanding and respect in your relationships with the people close to you in your life. Friends and family will have a better hold on how you'd like to be treated and also be more aware of how much and what they can expect of you.

Communicating your needs, especially concerning your time, will help you nurture your friendships and other relationships. Making time for people shows them that you value and appreciate them. Being fully present during that time shows that you respect and care for them. If you're constantly answering work calls or checking your emails, you're sending a message to people that they're not important to you and that you don't treasure getting to be with them.

Something that someone does might upset you, but if you haven't made them aware of it, they won't know. Instead, they will continue to repeat the behavior, leading to you resenting them. You can easily avoid things like this by clearly asserting your boundaries and making people aware not to overstep them. Doing this means you can communicate more effectively with those around you. You'll also be better at expressing your needs and wants, which will lead to happier dynamics and less conflict.

When you have personal boundaries in place, you free up time for self-care. This means you get to set aside time just for yourself that's free from the demands of work or the expectations of other people. You can focus on your own wants and needs and do things that make you happy. Having this time to rest and relax will also reduce stress and anxiety and improve your mental and emotional well-being.

Professional Boundaries

Professional boundaries are the key to a healthier, more productive work environment. Setting clear expectations will ensure a more harmonious atmosphere and increased job satisfaction, especially when you work in a team.

When it comes to the professional sphere, one of the best things you can do for yourself is to learn how to say no. Decline requests to stay on after hours to finish a project or to take on additional tasks when you're already inundated with work. Setting boundaries regarding your hours is important for the sake of your own well-being. Making it clear that you're not available for work-related communications outside of these hours will protect your personal and social life from being overrun by your job.

These boundaries also extend to your workplace relationships. Everybody has experienced an overfamiliar colleague who overshares about themselves. Establishing the limitations of office interactions will allow you to be able to respectfully excuse yourself from such conversations without appearing rude. When you set boundaries with your colleagues, they know to keep your interactions strictly professional and not to pressure you for personal information. Having clear distinctions between these important spheres of your life will help you keep your professional and personal life separate. It will also allow you to use your work time to focus on the tasks you need to complete instead of wasting it gossiping about things that are unrelated to your job.

Boundary Myths and Misconceptions

Earlier, I shared with you how my lack of understanding about boundaries kept me from embarking on the same transformational journey you're now on. I've since found that I was not alone in these beliefs! Many people have similar misconceptions, and you may have them, too. Below are some of the most common myths. Let's dispel the misinterpretations that might be holding you back so that you can free yourself to reap the great benefits of healthy interactions.

Boundaries Are Selfish

This was a big one for me. I thought that putting up walls made me a bad friend, daughter, sister, and employee. I thought I had to agree to everything that people asked of me if I were to be a positive part of their lives. The truth is that sometimes saying yes is the more selfish act. If you consent to things just to make others happy, you are being disingenuous to those people.

Boundaries are not selfish—they are a form of self-care. When you put up barriers, you create the opportunity to grow and develop yourself. When you're the best version of yourself, you will be better to other people. You do not have an unlimited reserve of energy to give away, and, at some point, you'll need to take time out to restore and replenish yourself. You avoid this happening in the first place by setting boundaries.

When you look after yourself and put your well-being first, you are showing up for others as the best version of yourself. That is the opposite of being selfish!

Boundaries Ruin Relationships

Setting boundaries in your relationships is like giving people an instruction manual on how to make you happy without them needing to figure it out through trial and error.

At first, the idea of changing the terms of your relationships with the people in your life might seem scary. Maybe you don't know how they'll react. It's normal to feel anxious about changing the dynamics of your pre-existing relationships, but boundaries work to make your interactions healthier, not worse.

You might think that setting boundaries will push people away, but they will actually help others get closer to you. When you communicate your needs, you're letting people know how you'd like them to treat you and how to make you feel safer and happier in your interactions with them. This will improve the quality of your relationships because your wants and needs are more likely to be met, and there will be fewer conflicts.

Boundaries Are Universal

There is no one-size-fits-all type of boundary. What works in one relationship might not necessarily work in another. You are allowed to adjust your terms to suit different circumstances. Boundaries are not set in stone; they are more of a guideline than an unchanging law. You are allowed to have different limits with different people, depending on what you're comfortable with. And you don't need to justify why you set certain conditions with one person and not with another. How much you're willing to give of yourself is a personal choice, and you don't owe anyone an explanation.

Personal Boundaries and Identity

Before you can begin the process of setting boundaries, you first need to be aware of which ones will best suit your needs. In order to do that, you need a good understanding of yourself. You need to be aware of what will work most effectively for you in your relationships, and that begins with knowing your wants and needs. You can gain an awareness of this through the act of self-reflection.

Boundaries and Self-Reflection

Self-reflection is a process that involves taking a step back to look at your thoughts, feelings, and actions. This will enable you to gain a deeper understanding of yourself and adopt a new perspective on your experiences. It is an important part of determining the nature of your relationships because it allows you to look at what your values are, discover your comfort levels, know your preferences, and learn what you need. By being introspective, you are more easily able to identify areas of your life where boundaries might be lacking or in need of improvement.

When you take a moment to reflect on yourself, you gain a deeper sense of self-awareness and can draw from your past experiences to make better, more informed decisions in the future.

If you're looking for some ways to practice self-reflection, you might like to try:

- journaling
- mindfulness meditation
- getting feedback from people you trust
- scheduling weekly time for self-reflection

Setting Personal Boundaries and Limits

After gaining a better understanding of yourself, you become more able to identify what will be effective for you.

When formulating your personal boundaries, take the following into consideration:

- **Your core values:** Taking a moment to consider the values, principles, and ethics by which you measure your actions and decisions is a good place to start. Being aware of these things will make it easier for you to set personal boundaries that align with who you are as a person.
- **Your emotional needs:** How would you like to be treated? Do you feel respected by others? How do

you need to be supported to feel secure in your relationships? What do you need for your emotional well-being?

- **Your physical limits:** Where do you draw the line when it comes to physical proximity with other people? How much privacy do you require in order to feel safe? What are your comfort levels with regard to physical touch?
- **Your work/life balance needs:** Consider what limitations you need to place on your work demands to enable yourself to still enjoy a healthy personal life. Think of the amount of time you need for yourself or what you would like to be doing outside of work.

The Role of Boundaries in Personal Development

Boundaries are an integral part of personal growth and development. The process of learning how to create and set them already implies such a deep sense of self-awareness, which provides a foundation upon which transformation can begin.

Before you can set boundaries, though, you first need to gain a deeper understanding of yourself. Like for many of us, it's likely not often that you'll take the time to pause and reflect on what your values and beliefs are and how they influence your decisions. When you start this journey into self-improvement, you are forced to take a long, hard look at yourself and consider how your lack of boundaries has contributed to your unhappiness.

Following this, you can then assess your needs and wants and find ways to create boundaries that align with them. Through this process, you will start gaining some self-confidence and improve your self-esteem. Learning to prioritize yourself isn't easy, and it might not come naturally, especially if you've been a people-pleaser for most of your life. However, setting limits permits you to do things for yourself. Spending time doing things you enjoy, taking time to relax— this too, is an act of growth.

When you begin to reaffirm your boundaries with others, you're teaching yourself that your needs matter, that your wants are important, and that you are worthy of respect. This, in turn, allows new people you encounter and those who are part of your life to see the same things. Slowly, you will see their behavior toward you changing. You might even start to see a shift in the way you see yourself. You'll no longer be a pushover who is unable to say no and unwilling to communicate your needs. Setting limits will empower you to find your voice and start using it to protect your mental and emotional well-being.

Conclusion

Now that you know what boundaries are, why they're important, and how to start identifying where you need to incorporate them, let's get you started on setting some of your own. In the next chapter, I'll show you how to effectively implement and communicate boundaries in your own life.

2. Identifying and Communicating Your Boundaries

Daring to set boundaries is about having the courage to love ourselves, even when we risk disappointing others.

— Brené Brown

Are there things that bother you in your relationships that you fail to communicate with others? Do you often overlook certain things, only to have them repeatedly resurface, leading to resentments? If so, you are suffering from the effects of a lack of boundaries in your life.

When I was younger, I had a best friend named Sally. She was incredibly smart, outgoing, and lively. Her laugh could fill a room, and her emotions were just as big and hard to ignore. Over time, though, I began to find her overly emotional nature somewhat of an annoyance; however, I failed to communicate this to her. Instead, I harbored resentment.

As time went on and my annoyance grew, I found that it was no longer something I could ignore or tolerate. I decided I had reached my limit. Still, I was afraid to tell Sally how I felt. Instead, I gradually distanced myself from our friendship and even started spreading negative rumors about her, which resulted in her being the target of bullying. This is still a source of deep shame for me.

Had I known back then what I know now, I would have handled the situation a lot better. I would have set an emotional boundary much earlier on. I wouldn't have allowed my frustration to escalate to the point that it did. If I had communicated with her, I would have been able to justify my decision to distance myself from her if she'd kept crossing my boundaries. I would also not have resorted to the tactics I did to sever a friendship I didn't have the guts to just break off at the time.

For me, this was a big lesson in the importance of not just having boundaries but in being able to communicate them effectively. I was so afraid to confront Sally with my feelings because I didn't want to hurt her. But, in the end, what I did was so much more hurtful than it would have been to just be honest and upfront from the beginning.

Moving forward with this example in mind, in this chapter, we'll be exploring ways that you can learn to identify what your boundaries are as well as communicate them with others. This will help you avoid finding yourself in situations like the one I ended up in with my friend.

Self-Discovery in Boundary Setting

In the previous chapter, we've spoken about how boundaries start with you and that before you can start to know what your needs are, you need to understand who you are. This can be a great journey of self-discovery where you begin to look at yourself in ways you never have before and see yourself from a new perspective. You might even be surprised by some of the things you learn!

Personal Values

Before you can decide what boundaries are important to you, consider your personal values. What are the things that shape who you are? What's important to you? Your core values are kind of like the rubric you use to assess your actions and decisions. They shape your attitude and determine the way you interpret the world around you and your experiences in it. They aren't set in stone either: They grow and change as you do, and they are impacted by your experiences as you learn.

Your values are like your moral compass, and your emotional and psychological well-being depends on your ability to live a life that aligns with your principles. With this in mind, you can understand why setting boundaries that are congruent with your beliefs is important.

Some examples of personal values are:

- integrity
- open-mindedness
- empathy

- authenticity
- ambition
- kindness
- recognition
- power
- success
- spirituality

There are as many diverse values as there are complex personalities in the world. Your ideals depend on your upbringing and experiences, both of which are what shapes them. Your core beliefs have a big influence on how you make decisions and interact with people. For example, a person who values success will accept a job that they don't enjoy if they believe it will satisfy their ambition. A person who values happiness might choose a job that pays less but that they'll enjoy more.

When you apply this thinking to boundary setting, you can see how people with different values might place more emphasis on certain types of boundaries than others. Deciding what you're willing to tolerate based on your beliefs is vital because it's the only way to ensure that your boundaries work for you and will give you the desired results.

Emotional Triggers

An emotional trigger is any topic or situation that makes you feel uneasy or uncomfortable. When you experience an intense reaction to something, it's because it's alerting you to an aspect of yourself or your life that you're not entirely happy with or might be ashamed of. It might also be a signal of a wound that you haven't healed from, so it could also be bringing up an unpleasant memory that you'd rather not deal with.

When you draw lines around these triggers, you're able to limit your exposure to situations that might upset you, and you protect your mental and emotional well-being. Learning what provokes emotional reactions from you can be an important aspect of your self-discovery journey. It may lead to you uncovering parts of yourself or your past that you'd never processed before.

If you're wondering how you can identify your emotional triggers, consider the following:

- **Do you have physical reactions as a result of trying to suppress your emotions?** When you've learned to try and suppress your emotional reactions instead of dealing with them, your body may react physically. This can take the form of shaking, having an elevated heart rate, crying, struggling to speak, or being unable to make eye contact. If you find yourself experiencing these symptoms in response to a situation, you might have been emotionally triggered.
- **What situation precipitated the physical response?** Did you have this reaction in response to something that was said? Did you see something that bothered you? Think about what was happening around the time you had the reaction.
- **Is there a pattern or a common thread to these emotional triggers?** When you reflect on other

situations where you experienced a similar reaction, what do they have in common? Do you find that you always respond this way when you feel unheard or criticized, for example? Try and spot the underlying pattern.

- **Do you find yourself experiencing these reactions around a particular person?** Upon reflection, can you think of a person who has always elicited this sort of emotional response from you? It could even be a certain group or type of people, such as authority figures. In other cases, the trigger may be tied to specific people. Maybe anytime someone brings up meeting their parents, you find yourself suddenly feeling on edge.

- **Are there any specific topics or situations that make you uncomfortable?** Sometimes, you may find yourself throwing out sarcastic remarks any time a particular subject comes up or getting defensive whenever someone tries to point out a mistake you've made. When you look at your reactions to people and events around you, you will often find clues as to what your emotional triggers might be.

Once you've become aware of your what sets you off, you're much more able to deal with it. One of the many ways you can begin to limit your exposure to potential triggers is to start setting boundaries. When you put up defense systems around people and situations that could potentially harm your emotional and mental well-being, you can protect yourself from the damage they can cause. You also give yourself the space you need to start healing the underlying trauma associated with those triggers once they're no longer actively bringing you harm.

Learning From Past Experiences and Relationships

About five years after the disastrous end of my friendship with Sally, I became close friends with a girl named Tammy. At first, she and I did everything together and were practically joined at the hip. Unfortunately, our relationship eventually began to follow the same emotionally turbulent pattern my friendship with Sally had. Once again, I found myself in a place where I was feeling overwhelmed by someone but unable to voice my discomfort out of fear.

Instead of communicating with Tammy and letting her know how I was feeling, I let resentment seep into our friendship. Instead of putting up a boundary, I allowed my feelings to create a rift between us, one we were never able to recover from. I realized much later that, had I only said something earlier, I could have continued to enjoy a relationship that had the potential to last a lifetime. It was my own failure to assert myself and express my feelings that led to me losing a lifelong friendship.

Following these two experiences with Sally and Tammy, I began to see how my behavior was holding me back socially. I took these unfortunate outcomes as lessons and used them to fuel my journey toward learning to set healthy boundaries in my friendships and being more open and honest in expressing my feelings. As a result, I now enjoy wholesome, fulfilling, and healthy relationships with all the close people in my life.

People are not stagnant. As we get older, we grow, and we learn. We can take hurtful experiences from our past and use them to better ourselves in the future. If not for the experiences I had earlier on in my life, I would not be enjoying the gratifying friendships I have now.

Communication Strategies

You've probably formed an idea of what boundaries you'd like to set. You've done self-reflection, you've figured out your values, and you've identified your emotional triggers. However, that's only the beginning! Knowing your boundaries is a great first step, but now you need to communicate them to others. A lot of people expect us to just know what their boundaries are or be able to guess. However, the only way you can make certain that your limits are respected is to clearly convey them to others.

This can seem daunting, and the prospect of having those conversations might seem frightening, but it's necessary. When you're open in how you communicate, you set clear expectations for the way you would like to be treated. After that, it's easier for you to address any issues that may arise as a result of people overstepping. Much like I learned with the issues I used to have with my friends, you also need to accept that you cannot resent someone for crossing a boundary you never made them aware of to begin with.

Let's look at ways you can begin communicating your boundaries with the people in your life:

Start Small

Since you're likely introducing new boundaries to existing relationships, remember to start small. People need to get used to the idea that there will be new rules guiding your interactions, so try not to bombard them with too much all at once. I know you're probably fired up to implement this new skill in all of your relationships but remember that this is a marathon, not a sprint. Taking your time to slowly begin establishing your boundaries with the people around you will give them time to adjust.

You can also get a better understanding of what works and what doesn't work if you take your time with how you start integrating barriers into your life. If you just suddenly inundate people with new terms for your interactions, you're more likely to receive a negative response. They may either feel attacked or that you're changing your relationship completely.

Be Assertive

When you communicate assertively, you are more direct and clearer about the point you're trying to get across. Be gentle and respectful in the way you communicate. This doesn't mean you need to be apologetic or back down; you can be firm while still being kind. Make sure you relay how you feel, why you've decided to set a particular boundary, and why it's important to you that it be respected.

Use statements referring to yourself to avoid people feeling blamed or attacked. When you use statements beginning with "I," you come across as more direct and assertive. You should also try and be specific when establishing the circumstances that have contributed to you needing the boundary so that people know not to repeat the offending behavior.

For example, if someone has been belittling you and it's bothering you, tell them: "I feel disrespected when you talk down to me, and I'd appreciate it if you'd refrain from doing that in the future."

Remember That "No" Is a Full Sentence

Learning to say no can be difficult, especially if you're not used to it. So often, we forget that we don't owe people explanations for our decisions and that "no" is a full sentence. This means that if someone asks you to do something, you can simply decline and leave it there. You don't need to justify your response or offer an explanation as to why.

Speak Up

Communicating boundaries isn't just about having a conversation about them. It's also about speaking up in moments where you previously would have let things go. If you're in a situation where you feel uncomfortable or you think that someone has crossed a line, speak up. Pointing these things out as they happen might make it easier for someone to understand your boundaries than sitting them down and rattling off a list. When you correct someone's behavior in real-time, they're immediately able to see where they might have offended you, and they can make a mental note not to do that again.

Speaking up might be difficult, especially in professional settings, but it's important for you to learn to use your voice.

Also, bear in mind that setting boundaries is a process that takes time. People might not get it at first, and you'll probably need to remind them once or twice that some areas are off limits. Point it out every time they cross that line and let them know that you're standing firm in your boundary.

Limit Your Availability

Communicating boundaries doesn't always need to be a verbal declaration. You can also use your actions, especially when it comes to people having access to you. Using digital features such as an automated email response outside of work hours or setting your phone to "do not disturb" when you'd like some time to yourself are some nonverbal methods you can use to communicate your boundaries. Additionally, you can put passwords on your devices and lock away personal items you don't want others using to limit how others use your belongings.

Be Consistent

The only way to ensure that people respect the boundaries you've set is for you to be consistent with them. If you've set a rule around something, make sure that you stick to it. When you're flaky around holding people accountable, they'll learn over time that they can do as they please. You also seem less firm in your convictions if you fail to enforce limits or remind people when they've overstepped. It will be hard at first, and you might feel uncomfortable having to point out when people have violated a boundary. You might even be tempted to let it slide for the time being, but that will be counterproductive.

Once you've made yourself a promise to start implementing safeguards, you need to commit to it. Not just for the sake of yourself but for the sake of your relationships. If you keep allowing others to cross your boundaries, your relationships will eventually fail because you'll feel disrespected and unhappy. You do yourself a disservice when you allow others to violate your needs, and you do them a disservice when you fail to alert them to the fact that they have.

Be Flexible

We've mentioned before how boundaries aren't set in stone and that, upon further reflection, it's perfectly okay to decide that certain ones aren't working for you. When you're learning something new, there will be a lot of trial and error involved, and that's alright. Maybe you weren't exactly sure how to carry out a particular boundary, and the method you used hasn't really worked out. You're allowed to backtrack and change to suit your ideal outcomes.

It's also okay to compromise. If you express a boundary to someone and they ask you to alter it in some small way, that makes it easier for them to respect it. Provided someone is not disregarding your needs entirely, you're allowed to establish ways that your limits can shift to accommodate other people.

Conclusion

The process of learning how to identify your boundaries and then finding ways to implement them is very much like finding your voice and then learning how to use it.

Through self-discovery, you've learned what's important to you and what makes you tick. You've gained self-awareness about your triggers and the best ways to avoid putting yourself in situations that might harm your mental health. Now that you know what you need to protect your peace, you can begin the journey to manifest that vision into your life.

You start by introducing boundaries into your relationships. That act in itself will empower you and boost your confidence. As you do this, you'll learn how to express your needs and create mutual respect in your relationships. You'll figure out where to draw the line when it comes to accommodating others and compromising, and you'll see that pleasing others should never come at the expense of your own happiness. You'll also realize that you can draw on the lessons from your negative past experiences and use what you've learned to improve your relationships in the future, just as I have.

By now you're probably feeling a bit more confident in your ability to create and set boundaries, but it's not all going to be smooth sailing. Sometimes, you may come across challenges when trying to set them, both with others and yourself. In the next chapter, we'll be discussing some of these potential challenges and exploring ways you can overcome them.

3. Overcoming Challenges in Setting Boundaries

Being your best is not so much about overcoming the barriers other people place in front of you as it is about overcoming the barriers we place in front of ourselves.

— Kieren Perkins

S etting boundaries isn't without its challenges. Sometimes, the only thing that's getting in the way of your happiness is you. Some of the obstacles you face might come from self-doubt, and feelings of guilt might become a stumbling block on your journey. A lack of self-esteem might tell you that you don't deserve to ask people to respect your needs or that your happiness isn't as important as the comfort of others. If you want to overcome these barriers to progress, you need to work through them.

Other times, the hurdles you face come from the people around you or societal pressure. It's difficult trying to navigate the process of introducing boundaries to your existing relationships, especially when you're afraid of losing people you care about as a result. You don't want to rock the boat by suddenly changing things from the way they've always been.

When you're raised a certain way or grow up in a certain culture, there are customs and expectations put in place that make it difficult for you to establish boundaries. When you draw a line and stand your ground, your parents or other elders might see it as an act of defiance or blatant disrespect. In these situations, redefining the terms of a relationship can be extremely difficult. It can bring a lot of attention and create conflict within them.

In this chapter, we'll address these difficulties by discussing how both internal and external factors may be obstacles in your boundary setting. We'll explore ways to navigate setbacks and overcome them, or at the very least, how you can find the best resolution in these situations.

Addressing Internal Hurdles

As someone who'd been a people pleaser for most of my life, the idea of setting any boundaries was terrifying to me. I had always avoided conflict and confrontation at all costs. The biggest cost, however, had always been to my own happiness and peace of mind.

The journey to overcoming these fears and anxieties began with acknowledging that I deserved to be content in my life and relationships. I had to realize that the people who cared about me would want me to be happy and would be willing to make small changes for me to be more comfortable with our interactions. It also, unfortunately, meant I had to learn to be okay with losing some relationships with people who weren't willing to allow me to grow.

Understanding Guilt

Having feelings of guilt when you begin to set boundaries is normal. You might feel selfish for having to ask people to change how they interact with you or for having to put your foot down. Addressing other people's behavior and treatment of you might make you feel like you're the villain, but you're not. There's nothing wrong with asking to be treated the way you want to be. In fact, people who care about you will be happy to make changes that allow you to feel happier in your relationships.

It's also important for you to remind yourself that boundaries aren't about hurting other people or pushing them away. They're a way for you to safeguard your own mental and emotional well-being. You're not attacking someone when you point out the things they do or say that upset you —you're simply showing them how their behavior has impacted you and allowing them to mend it.

Focus on the pure intentions behind your decision to express your needs whenever guilt comes up. Boundaries don't come from a place of anger or malice but from a genuine attempt to improve your relationships with the people around you.

Overcoming Fear

It's understandable to experience fear or anxiety when you're about to do something you've never done before, and setting boundaries for the first time is no exception. You might be afraid to take this measure with people because you don't know how they'll react, or you think they might cut you out of their lives. Other factors can also contribute to your fear, such as your culture or upbringing, low self-esteem, or negative past experiences. Allowing these fears to stop you, however, would be doing yourself a disservice.

The best way to overcome your fear is to practice communicating more assertively. Maybe you can rehearse what you're going to say before you have the conversation. If your people-pleasing nature is what's causing anxiety, remember that other people's reactions to your limits are not your responsibility. If someone isn't willing to show you respect, then that says more about them than it does about your boundaries.

Emotional Resilience

Emotional resilience is your ability to cope with and handle overwhelming situations and adapt to changing circumstances. Without boundaries, your ability to be resolute is greatly diminished. If you can't put up boundaries to protect yourself when things get to be too much for you, you'll end up feeling depleted and burnt out.

We all have a set amount of energy to give, and when we don't have limits on how we allocate it, we end up giving all of it away to others. This means that, when the chips are down, you don't have any left for yourself and that you'll never have any energy to dedicate to the things that are important to you. In order to build your emotional resilience, you need to be able to protect your reserves from being depleted by other people. The only way to do this is to express your needs.

Learning to say no when you need to allows you to preserve your energy and use it where it's needed instead of giving it away at every request. When you can do that, you'll find it easier to cope with your life stressors and empower yourself to adapt when things don't go as expected.

Handling Personal Barriers and Self-Imposed Limits

You might be dealing with some internal barriers that are keeping you from setting boundaries. These can include being afraid of how people may respond if you speak up about an issue you've always let slide. Or maybe you're not entirely sure what boundaries you need and how you can best express them in words. Sometimes, there's just that little voice in your head that's telling you not to rock the boat, or that you don't have a right to ask this of people, or that you don't deserve to have your desires met.

The first thing you need to do is recognize these thoughts as barriers that you're creating for yourself. The truth is that you don't know how people are going to react—the only way to know for sure is to actually do it. Sitting around dreaming up a thousand different scenarios isn't going to benefit you, and it's likely never going to go as badly as you imagine it will. You also need to release yourself from the responsibility of other people's thoughts and opinions. What they think about your boundaries is not your concern. You are not taking the action for them. You are doing it for you.

Navigating External Challenges

The obstacles we face when it comes to setting boundaries may come from the people around us, and this can be a lot more complicated to deal with. As much as we may want to respect our friends, family, or coworkers, it's imperative for our mental health and well-being that we find ways to still have our boundaries acknowledged, at the very least. So, let's look at some common external challenges you might come across and how to overcome them.

Societal and Cultural Influences

The culture in which you're raised plays a big role in your perceptions and interpretation of the world and your place in it. In some cultures, emphasis is placed on the importance of family. Along with this comes expectations of sacrifice, honor, and loyalty. Having boundaries becomes nearly impossible because you're almost always expected to place what's good for the family as a whole above your wants and needs. Trying to put up boundaries or saying no to requests would be seen as extremely rude, selfish, and disrespectful.

Furthermore, traditional cultures have a firm belief in respecting the authority of elders. This would make it incredibly difficult for someone to reject instructions based on their level of personal comfort or preferences. Culturally, they'd be expected to obey without question when someone of an older generation asks something of them. The concept of personal boundaries is nonexistent.

When you come from a traditional family, the choice to stand your ground may result in you alienating yourself from your family. It can have a detrimental impact on your relationships, and family members may even start excluding you from group events and special occasions. At some point, you'll need to decide to either stay true to yourself and not relent to their pressure or cave in and relinquish your boundaries. It's not always easy to know what the right choice is in these situations, especially when it becomes clear that you can't have it both ways.

Here's one example of how our upbringing can harm us when we don't draw limits to protect ourselves:

I once read a story about a girl who was often treated in the ER for a severe allergic reaction to shellfish. After a few visits, the doctors tending to her had noticed a pattern in her admissions and that they appeared to happen around the same time of the month. As you can imagine, this was a source of great concern to them, as these incidents can be fatal in some cases.

Upon further investigation, hospital staff discovered that, once a month, her father prepared a dish containing shellfish for his family, and the girl didn't have a choice about eating it. Because her caretakers didn't believe her assertions that she had an intolerance, despite her numerous hospitalizations, she was forced to eat the dish that had been prepared. To her elders, sharing in the meal was a show of respect for his authority and a sign of appreciation. Despite knowing what would happen to her, she dutifully did what was expected of her.

For me, this story is a harsh example of how cultural pressure can negatively impact a person's ability to enforce a boundary, even when it could save their life.

Family Dynamics and Relationship Pressures

Growing up, I had an aunt who had a background in education and who was employed as an English teacher. Fortunately for me, she taught me the language for free, starting when I was of a young age. It's thanks to these lessons that I was able to grasp it so easily in later years. However, this act of kindness was one that would come to haunt me.

My grandmother held my aunt's generosity over my head for years to come. She would often remind me that it was only thanks to my family that I was so proficient and that, as a show of my gratitude, I ought to help my aunt in any way that she required or requested. Although she had never mentioned this herself, the traditional mindset put me in a position where I felt indebted to her.

Duty-bound, I would go out of my way to grant whatever she requested, even at great personal cost to myself and at the expense of my wants and needs. For many years, I felt that I was unable to refuse whenever my aunt asked for help. Although she never called on me for anything substantial, on the odd occasion that I would try and refuse, my grandmother was always quick to remind me of the kindness I was indebted to.

These feelings of guilt and resentment began to build up over the years, eating away at our relationship. As time went on, the love and respect I'd previously had for both my aunt and grandmother slowly faded away. I found myself distancing myself from them, avoiding their calls and not visiting them as often as I once had. I missed out on years I could have spent making cherished memories with them. Eventually, my grandmother passed away and my aunt moved abroad.

In hindsight, I wish I'd had the courage back then to set firm boundaries within my familial relationships. If I'd stood my ground and not allowed myself to be emotionally black-mailed, I would have been so much happier.

Professional Challenges

Often, we find ourselves in professional situations where those in positions of authority abuse their power by over-stepping our boundaries. All the while they know that we won't say anything because we don't want to lose our jobs. In these cases, it might be helpful for you to approach HR with your concerns and ask them for advice on how best to handle the situation.

Setting boundaries in the workplace might be difficult, especially when you consider the corporate hierarchy. There will be times when the person you need to set boundaries with is in a higher position than you, which gives them an unfair position of power over you that they might exploit. Setting up boundaries with them may feel like a bad decision for your career prospects.

You might fear expressing discomfort with your manager, for example, for fear of losing your job or not being treated fairly. In other instances, you might want to stay in your boss's good books because you're hoping for a promotion or an increase in your salary.

Digital Challenges

Living in a digital world is both a blessing and a curse. Suddenly, people have access to us at all times of the day, and they expect us to be available to answer their calls and emails at the drop of a hat.

You may have communicated your desire to disconnect from work outside of office hours, but that doesn't necessarily mean that your colleagues are going to respect your wishes. Sometimes, you may be the one who falters because you find it tempting to take a peek at your work emails over the weekend, especially when you see a notification popping up on your phone.

The first step to setting digital boundaries, then, is self-discipline. If you can't adhere to your own rules, other people won't either. If it's too difficult for you to ignore them at first, turn off your notifications or set your phone to silent when you need time away from endless work communications. As time goes on, people will begin to realize that you won't engage with them or respond after hours, which will make them more likely to respect your limits.

If, however, you're always caving and answering their phone calls or responding to their emails despite asserting that you don't wish to be contacted outside of office hours, they'll get used to the idea that this request is optional, and you'll find it extremely difficult to enforce it going forward.

Conclusion

By the closing of this chapter, you will have delved deep within yourself to figure out what boundaries you need to set in your life in order to feel respected and be treated the way you want to be. You've gained confidence in your ability to communicate this to the people in your life in a way that won't tarnish or negatively impact your existing relationships. You've also overcome obstacles, both internal and external, on your journey to setting these boundaries.

Now that you have these boundaries in place, you need to learn how to keep them there. The next step we're going to be exploring is how to maintain and adapt your boundaries. After all, life is ever-changing, and what you need to feel fulfilled in your relationships now won't be the same as what you may need years from now. Adjusting your boundaries to suit your changing needs is therefore an important skill to learn. We'll be exploring this further in the next chapter.

4. Maintaining and Adapting Boundaries

Each time you set a healthy boundary, you say "yes" to more freedom.

— Nancy Levin

D id you know that the benefits of boundaries are backed up by science? Studies have proven that young people who learn how to set clear, consistent boundaries grow up to become healthier adults than those who don't (*Boundaries & Expectations*, n.d.).

This fact further proves that being consistent in upholding your boundaries is essential. When you fail to be persistent in this, you give people the impression that you're not serious about your limits, or that respecting them is optional. This will result in the lines you draw being violated often, and it will leave you feeling worse off than if you hadn't established them at all.

Being consistent with maintaining the measures you've decided on to protect yourself, your time, and your energy involves verbally communicating them and then reinforcing them through your actions. This means that if you've told a coworker that you won't be available to take their call after hours and they contact you anyway, you ignore them. By doing this, you make it clear to people that your boundaries are not negotiable and that you won't be pressured into relenting or going back on what you've decided.

We've already spoken about how boundaries are not set in stone, and this is true for many reasons. For one, the ones you set in one aspect of your life may not necessarily translate well across the board. That is to say, the limits you have with close family members won't be the same as those you have with your colleagues. Your needs are dependent on the situation as well as the nature of the relationship you have with the person you're putting up a barrier with.

Another reason why it's important to be adaptable is because your needs and wants will change as you grow. If you're flexible, you'll be able to reassess your boundaries over time and tweak them to suit where you are in your life. Sometimes, you may find that what you thought would be effective doesn't actually meet your needs the way you thought it would. In these cases, you need to be flexible enough to realize that you should change the limit to one that better fulfills your desires or needs.

To help you manage this challenge, this chapter will explore the ways you might need to change and adapt your bound-

aries. As you discover yourself and gain a better understanding of what's important to you, these new
developments must be reflected in the way you approach
your relationships. The lines you draw to protect yourself
should nurture and enhance your growth, as well as support
your ability to communicate and express your needs to the
people around you.

Consistency and Adaptability

When you first look at the words "consistency" and "adaptability," you might think they're opposites. On the surface,
that may be the case, but they're actually two sides of the
same coin.

Consistency is about not giving up and putting in the time
and effort to get to where you want to be. When it comes to
boundaries, this means you hold firm to your principles,
despite how others may perceive or react to them.
Regardless of whether or not people choose to respect them
or follow them, you need to stick to your guns.

As you remain consistent in your stance, you'll see people
come to respect your limits over time. Being persistent
shows them that you're serious and that you know what you
want. It proves to them that you will not be persuaded or
manipulated into changing your mind. It speaks volumes of
your determination when you're able to hold onto your
boundaries, no matter what. Even if people don't respect the
measure, they'll respect your consistency.

On the other hand, adaptability is about being flexible and
able to alter your views to suit changing circumstances.

When upholding the terms of how you want to be treated, this might initially feel counterintuitive, but it's not. Being adaptable doesn't mean you have a boundary one moment and then cast it aside the next. It just means you're able to compromise on the specifics for the sake of making it more suitable for your needs. You're still consistent in what you're asking for, but you're changing the method by which you're receiving it.

When it comes to setting boundaries, the combination of these two qualities is invaluable because it will give you the ability to set firm boundaries, make sure they're being respected by others, and ensure your needs are being met despite changing circumstances. When it comes to the long-term maintenance of your boundaries, these two skills will get you a long way.

Maintaining Your Boundaries

Sometimes, it might feel like setting the boundaries was the easy part because maintaining them is so much harder. That initial sense of achievement you felt when you finally found your voice and communicated your needs with the people around you wears off over time. You may find that, although others appeared receptive to what you had to say, they continued treating you the same way afterward, as if that conversation hadn't happened. In those cases, it's easy to feel downhearted and to want to give up altogether. But this is where the importance of consistency comes in.

You found the courage to speak up and tell people how you'd like to be treated; now, you need to hold them to it. Maintaining your boundaries is about following up your words with actions. Don't let things slide or sweep violations under the rug. Call people out when they fail to respect you and keep doing it, no matter how many times you need to repeat yourself.

Remind yourself why you set the boundaries to begin with. The discomfort and annoyance of repeating the same thing over and over is a small price to pay for your mental peace and emotional well-being.

If you're looking for some helpful tips on staying consistent, here are some things you can consider:

- When the situation becomes uncomfortable, remind yourself of the force that drove you to set the boundary. Instead of sitting in the discomfort of other people's reactions, remind yourself of the emotional benefits you'll gain from having your needs respected.
- Be compassionate but don't be a pushover. This means that you can have a certain amount of understanding when people accidentally violate a boundary, but you still need to reinforce it. If they continue to disrespect it, you need to consider following up with consequences.
- Learn to compromise. You don't need to discard a boundary altogether, but you can be flexible when it comes to making adjustments to make it more agreeable to the situation you're in at the time.

Adapting Boundaries to Life Changes and Different Life Stages

An important aspect of setting healthy boundaries is knowing when you need to adapt them to suit your changing needs. If you see them as static and unchanging, they might end up doing you more harm than good. This is because they will end up limiting your opportunities for growth in different aspects of your life.

For example, if you have boundaries around how much time you spend with your family and then you have a baby, you will need to adjust your priorities. If you don't, you'll lose out on valuable quality time you could be spending creating a bond and connection with your newborn. Another example is if you have a digital boundary regarding not taking personal phone calls during work hours, but you have a sick parent—in that circumstance, you'll need to adapt that rule. Ignoring a call during this time could lead to you missing an emergency where you're needed at home.

As you grow and your relationships and priorities change, so should the limits you have with others and around how you allocate your time and energy. Remember, your boundaries are for you. They are a way for you to ensure that you feel respected in your relationships, that your values are being upheld, and that your needs are being met. The things that are most important to you will change over time and so will the things that make you feel respected within your relationships. It's okay for your boundaries to adapt to reflect these changes within yourself.

Adaptability doesn't mean compromising your happiness for the sake of other people's comfort. A change in your boundaries should never leave you worse off than you were before. Instead, these adjustments should enhance your experiences and improve your overall quality of life.

Re-Evaluating Your Boundaries

There are times when you need to pause and reflect on your current boundaries and consider whether or not they're effectively working for you the way you want them to. In some cases, you might be unsure whether you need to adapt to suit your current circumstances or if you need to stand your ground and not budge.

It's important to re-evaluate your values and principles regularly, especially if you're going through a time of great personal changes or the dynamics within your relationships have shifted. For example, you might feel a lot closer to a friend now than you did previously. So, you may decide to be a bit more flexible with how much you're willing to share with them; as a pair, you may be more open to allowing each other to reveal more personal information than you did before. Or perhaps your romantic relationship has progressed from one of casual dating to something more serious, and you'd like to reassess how far you let your partner in.

There are many reasons why you may feel the need to reassess your boundaries, and it doesn't only need to be as a result of changes happening in your life. Maybe you'd just like to see if the measures you currently have in place are having the desired outcomes in your relationships. Perhaps you feel like some of them have been ineffective and that you need to try a different approach. If you find that a particular line is constantly being crossed, maybe you need to take another look at how you communicated it and if it was understood.

When it comes to violations and reinforcing boundaries, you may find that repeatedly reminding the offending person of the fact that they're disrespecting you isn't enough. In this case, you need to start following up with consequences. Defining how you would like to be treated has a way of showing you the unhealthy relationships you might have in your life and revealing the people who are either unwilling to respect you or unable to meet your needs.

Always remember that the boundaries you put in place are there to improve your life, not make it more challenging. You are not obligated to compromise who you are for the sake of someone else's comfort. Instead of making yourself uncomfortable to accommodate people who don't respect your needs, consider limiting your interactions with those people or avoiding them altogether.

It's okay to adjust your boundaries if:

- your needs have changed
- your priorities have shifted
- your current boundaries have resulted in undesirable consequences
- your level of connection with someone has changed

It's not advisable to adjust your boundaries if:

- you feel like you're being pressured or manipulated into changing them

- doing so will put your mental or emotional well-being at risk
- people are consistently violating and disrespecting the boundaries you've set

Boundaries and Personal Growth

It's really no surprise that I experienced the period of my most exponential personal growth after learning to set boundaries. I'd spent so long watering other people's gardens, nurturing them so that they could flourish, that I'd neglected my own plants and my flowers had begun to wilt and die.

As soon as I started placing limits on how much of myself I was willing to sacrifice for the sake of others, I found that I suddenly had all this time and energy to dedicate to nourishing myself. It was the most empowering act of self-love I could have ever decided on. By simply realizing that I was worthy of the same time, love, and attention I so easily gave away, I allowed myself to embrace my journey and begin a process of self-discovery that ultimately led to healthier, more fulfilling relationships with the people around me.

Boundaries as Catalysts for Self-Discovery and Self-Esteem

When you set boundaries, you are limiting the number of external influences that you give your energy to, freeing it up to use on things that are important to you. When your boundaries align with your values, you feel more fulfilled and more at peace. Every time you decline to do something that doesn't feed your growth, you're agreeing to an opportunity that will build you up and help you thrive.

Boundaries also increase your level of self-esteem. The more you assert that your wants and needs are as important as those of others, the more you'll see yourself as worthy and capable of the same level of respect you show to them. You empower yourself every time you choose to put yourself first, and through the process of communicating your needs, you are finding your voice.

By going through this process myself, I realized that I had never before been able to express what I wanted or needed. I'd always felt too ashamed or shy to tell people how I'd like to be treated. As a result, I often felt like a pushover or a doormat. I'd spent so long putting others first that I felt beneath them, or that I was less than them. By asserting myself, I began the process of taking my power back. I gave myself the ability to take ownership of the things that were important to me without feeling apologetic about it. I permitted myself to take up space in this world instead of constantly shying away. Over time, I noticed myself becoming more confident and more vocal than I'd been before.

By taking time to reflect on my values and beliefs and how I could articulate boundaries that reflected them, I gained a new level of understanding of myself and what I stood for. Being able to conceptualize my principles strengthened my conviction in them and made it easier for me to communicate them with confidence and self-assuredness. This made it more impactful when I expressed my views to others and, in turn, it made them more willing to accept and respect my wishes.

I didn't just learn what boundaries I needed and how to set them. I learned who I was and what I stood for. I learned how to communicate assertively and respectfully and how to be firm in my stance. These new skills translated into a ripple effect that improved my overall communication in every other aspect of my life, including my relationships. It was the simple act of deciding to preserve some of the energy I was giving away and keep it for myself—the decision to dedicate a portion of myself to the things that mattered to me—that ended up making all the difference in the world.

Expanding Comfort Zones and Personal Horizons

We've mentioned that boundaries are not walls that you create around yourself to keep other people out, and they're also not a prison cell that keeps you locked in. It's great to have them in place because they empower you to know where your limits are and the most comfortable way for you to go about your life and be present in your relationships and interactions. However, that doesn't mean you need to stay within those confines.

On the contrary, allowing yourself to push yourself is one of the best ways for you to grow. The space you exist in within your boundaries is your comfort zone, and very little growth can happen while you're there. As tempting as it can be to go through life never stepping out of this designated safe zone, you will be hindering yourself if you never venture beyond that point.

Expanding your safety net isn't about firing yourself up to overlook things that make you extremely uncomfortable. It simply means giving yourself a little nudge to try new things and explore the unknown. It's entirely possible to push your boundaries without driving yourself over the edge. The great thing about knowing exactly what your limits are is that you'll always know how to get yourself back to a place where you feel safe. You don't need to do anything drastic or make any huge changes. You can start by taking baby steps into unchartered territory. With every small adventure you take outside your comfort zone, you're actually opening up to new horizons and widening your limits.

Conclusion

In this chapter, you've learned that maintaining boundaries isn't about sitting like a sentry guard outside palace walls and making sure that everything stays exactly as it's always been. Instead, if you want to maintain healthy relationships, you need to ensure that the limits you have are growing and changing as you do. Regularly reassess the measures you've put in place to protect your peace of mind and be flexible enough to realize when it's time for some revision. Boundaries are meant to improve your life and enhance your experiences, not stifle you and make you feel trapped.

You've seen that, once you're sure of yourself and what you're comfortable with and when you feel confident in your boundaries, then it's time to start exploring outside of them. Taking the risk and stepping outside of your comfort zone is the best way to expand your horizons and push yourself forward. You'll find that the more often you allow yourself to try new things and have new experiences, the more expansive your world becomes and the more your comfort zone expands.

Now that we've familiarized ourselves with boundaries in a general context, let's focus more on a few key areas where having healthy boundaries is of the utmost importance. These are areas of life such as the professional space, the digital domain, and the realm of self-care. More on these in the following chapter.

5. Special Focus Areas in Setting Boundaries

The hardest part about setting boundaries with people, no matter who they are, is not feeling confident in our authority to do so. As long as you realize that setting boundaries is necessary for healthy relationships, you will feel better defining and keeping them.

— Tamera Mowry-Housley

I moved to the United States in early 2020 and eagerly anticipated receiving my work authorization before landing my first job. The paperwork took nearly nine months to clear, which obviously caused me a great deal of anxiety. I wasn't entirely sure about my career goals and aspirations, but, after almost a year of unemployment, I was pretty eager to enter the workforce and start earning an income.

There were other challenges, though. For example, due to not having my own form of transportation, I was forced to walk or rely on Uber to get to work. This posed a challenge, especially during winter, given the long distances I needed to travel.

Desperate for any chance at employment, I found myself applying for literally any job posting I came across online, going so far as to consider a gas station job that offered a measly $10 an hour due to its close proximity to where I was living at the time. However, I was still unable to work until I received my Social Security card, which, at that point, was still a work in progress.

As luck would have it, a company nearby eventually emailed me, inviting me to apply for an entry-level recruitment position. I set up the interview and subsequently got the job. I was over the moon! Not only were they located only five miles away, but they were also a family-run business, and everyone there was very kind and accommodating. The owners treated us like family, and I felt so at ease with them that I began blurring professional lines, opening up to them about personal issues I was facing in my marriage. Despite our religious differences, I found myself building a close connection with my boss and his wife and had a sense of curiosity about their culture.

As you may have guessed, I had yet to learn the importance of having limits about what I shared and how open I allowed others to be with me. My lack of boundaries later came back to haunt me in the form of an unsettling revelation from my boss.

He expressed to me in a manner that made it sound like a prophecy that he believed my marriage would end in divorce. I was stunned by his comment and rather taken aback. I wasn't sure how to even respond. It was at that moment that I became aware that I had made a mistake by clouding the lines between personal and professional relationships.

This experience taught me the importance of establishing clear boundaries in the workplace. To help you avoid making the same mistakes, we'll be using this chapter to take a closer look at why it's vital to set up boundaries in the workplace, both physically and digitally. We'll also look at how these safeguards correlate to self-care practices and how we can use boundaries to protect our mental peace and emotional well-being.

Boundaries at Work

Setting healthy boundaries in professional spaces is an essential factor in having a good work-life balance. When you have and maintain strong principles in this domain, you're less likely to find yourself constantly sacrificing what matters in your personal life for the sake of your job. The limits you put in place aren't just about keeping your work and home lives separate—they also contribute to your overall sense of satisfaction and can increase your productivity and workflow.

Some of the many benefits of setting boundaries at work are that:

- They allow you to focus more on your tasks, which will increase your productivity.
- They decrease your stress levels by helping you manage workplace-related issues.
- They keep your workload manageable by not allowing you to take on more work than you can handle.
- They reduce your risk of burnout by helping you maintain a reasonable workload and reducing work-related stress.

As you can see, setting boundaries at work can make your job a lot easier for you. You'll be able to communicate with your colleagues and superiors about how much work you can reasonably handle, and you'll avoid people-pleasing behaviors like agreeing to do things when you actually don't have the time to. This will free you up to give all your attention to the tasks you need to be doing, enabling you to give them your best effort.

When you have firm professional boundaries with your colleagues, you're less likely to be distracted from your work by unnecessary personal issues that may come up. You'll also be able to keep your work from extending into your home life by setting restrictions around your hours.

The secret to job satisfaction isn't always having less work or working longer hours. It can sometimes be a simple matter of realizing your limits, communicating them, and maintaining them.

Types of Workplace Boundaries

There are three types of workplace boundaries that you'll probably find to be the most effective. Let's take a look at each of them:

Physical Boundaries

Physical boundaries at work can dictate the level of contact you're comfortable having with your colleagues. It can be small things like reaching out for a handshake when someone goes in for a hug. Creating this barrier might help reinforce the idea of a strictly professional relationship. Another measure you can take, if you're constantly disrupted, is using headphones to relay a message that informs your coworkers that you're busy and unable to engage with them.

You can also have physical boundaries concerning your possessions. For example, should a colleague ask to borrow something from you, no matter how small, you can allocate a set timeframe during which they can use it and request that they return it immediately afterward. If they don't, remind them of their promise and hold them accountable. This will prevent people from taking advantage of you by simply taking and never returning your personal belongings.

Emotional Boundaries

Setting emotional boundaries at work is important because it allows you to disengage from your colleagues' negative states without losing your ability to be empathetic. An example of this is to give someone space if you can see they're in a bad mood, especially when you know they want you to indulge them in it. This allows you to keep their energy from negatively impacting your day, but it also gives them the space to work through whatever they're going through on their own. Engaging with negative attitudes feeds into them, and they end up either rubbing off on you or harming you, both of which can affect your productivity and concentration.

Mental Boundaries

Having mental boundaries at work allows you to focus on what you need to get done and not fall prey to distractions. They can be implemented in different ways. One method is to clearly establish the hours that you will work and make it clear that you won't be doing any job-related activities outside of that time.

Mental boundaries will also protect you from being sucked into office gossip. Making it clear that you won't participate in such conversations and don't wish to be made a part of them will help you focus on your job and not waste time entertaining workplace politics.

Balancing Ambition and Self-Care

We all want to succeed, but that success comes with sacrifice. However, one of the things you should never sacrifice for the sake of ambition is your mental and emotional well-being. In the drive to achieve your goals, it's important to remember not to neglect yourself. Boundaries can play a vital role in balancing out your aspirations with your need for self-care.

When you set and implement healthy professional boundaries, you safeguard your mental well-being. Knowing where your limits are will help you understand when you're pushing yourself too hard and when you need to give yourself a break. The lines you draw at work will keep your ambition from getting the better of you when it comes to things like taking on more than you can handle or overworking yourself.

Remember, burnout is a very real possibility when you neglect your health for the sake of your goals. Working hard doesn't always mean doing more or keeping at it for longer. It can mean focusing on the tasks you need to do and fulfilling them to the best of your ability. Having strong and healthy professional boundaries will enable you to do just that.

Communication and Leadership in Boundary Setting

When it comes to being a leader, drawing a line between work and yourself also sets an example that others can follow. When you're in a position of authority and have healthy boundaries, the people below you learn that they can also determine their limits, and it fosters an atmosphere of mutual growth and respect.

A leader without boundaries is difficult to trust. Your team won't be sure how to approach or work with you because you haven't set the standard for how they should. By establishing these guidelines, you also instill a sense of confidence in your authority. Those who report to you gain a clearer understanding of what is and isn't acceptable, and it reduces misunderstandings and conflicts in the workplace.

As a person with authority, it's your responsibility to model the appropriate behavior that you expect your subordinates to follow. When you're assertive, respectful, and kind in how you communicate the times you're available and how you expect to be treated, you create an atmosphere where others will do the same. This will make overall workflow more efficient, increase job satisfaction, and encourage effective communication.

It's also important for you to remember that if you want others to respect your boundaries, you also need to respect theirs. If you want your team to run smoothly, you need to be able to accept and respect their limitations. Be compassionate when they express this and be flexible when it comes to creating compromises for the sake of meeting each member's individual needs and acknowledging their core beliefs.

Digital Boundaries

In today's world, it's nearly impossible to live without technology. So much of what we do and how we interact takes place online. But don't you just hate it when you're trying to speak to someone and their eyes stay glued to their phone? That's why it's essential that you set digital boundaries for yourself.

Like with anything else, if you fail to set limits to how available you are online, you risk having it bleed into other areas of your life, too. Monitoring when and how often you use your phone, for example, is an important way to keep your digital life from seeping into your interpersonal interactions.

Navigating Social Media and Digital Communication

It's almost hard to imagine a time without social media. The many apps we use have become such an integral part of our lives and social interactions that it's easy to forget there was a time before any of them. Yet now that we've all started understanding the impact of our digital footprint, it's important that to know how to manage our online presence.

There are several strategies you can use to establish healthy boundaries online:

Limit Your Time

Allocate a set amount of time or schedule a specific time slot during the day when you engage with social media. This can be during your lunch break at work or while you're waiting for dinner to cook in the evening. Turn off your notifications outside of this time to make it less tempting to keep checking your social media apps.

Limit Your Consumption

I know I've personally fallen prey to the addictive nature of scrolling many times. The apps for social media platforms are designed to keep you engrossed so that you waste hours of your day scrolling through your feeds. To reduce this risk, set a limit for the amount of time you're allowed to spend online. Remember that you can control what you expose yourself to. If you find that a particular page or type of content is consistently upsetting you, mute it. Block it from your account so that you don't have to see it on your screen. Setting boundaries like this will help protect your mental peace.

Limit Your Access

Privacy and security are of the utmost importance when it comes to what you put online. Make sure you know what your privacy settings are so that you know who has access to your content. You never know who's seeing what you share when your posts are set to public, and you might be unnecessarily exposing yourself to harmful people and negative experiences. It's also important for you to have restrictions concerning what you post online. Never share personal information or anything about yourself that someone could use to bring you harm. Also, be aware of scammers and never share any financial information online.

Limit Your Engagement

A lot of people hide behind the anonymity of the internet to cause emotional harm to others. So, be conscious of how you engage with other users. Treat them as you would if you were interacting with them in real life. Avoid leaving negative or unkind comments or opinions about others. Don't hop onto bandwagons when you see other people engaging in cyberbullying. And, if you fall prey to it, ignore it. When you respond, you're giving those people what they want. It's not necessary to engage with every comment, response, or message that you receive online, just as you're not forced to interact with each person you meet in real life. Make sure that your conduct is an accurate representation of who you are as a person.

Digital Privacy and Mental Health

Speaking from personal experience, creating boundaries with regard to what you expose yourself to online can have a massive impact on your mental health and emotional well-being.

I used to follow several prominent influencers. I loved reading about their lives and seeing their experiences. As time went on, though, I began to feel poorly about my own life. I started comparing how I looked to their heavily photoshopped images and felt inadequate about my achievements whenever I saw them boasting of their accomplishments. I felt like my life paled in comparison to theirs and suddenly became dissatisfied with myself. I saw them traveling the world and buying expensive clothes and became disillusioned with my own existence.

Eventually, I came to see the toxic effect that religiously following these accounts was having on my mental peace, so I made the decision to unfollow all of those pages. As time went on, I saw my mindset begin to take a turn for the better.

Oftentimes, we're oblivious to how much of an impact the content we expose ourselves to can have on our self-image and sense of self-worth. Take time to reflect on how the pages you follow make you feel. Do they inspire you to become a better person, or do they make you feel like the person you are isn't enough? If it's the latter, you might want to reconsider who you're following.

You should always surround yourself with people and experiences that leave you feeling more positive and uplifted, on \d offline. I found that when I filled my feed with motivational posts and content for some fun hobbies that I enjoy, my feelings after engaging with social apps increased drastically.

Remember, you have control over who you follow, and you get to decide what is visible to you. Curate your feed so that it builds you up rather than breaks you down. Doing this allows you to keep protecting your mental and emotional well-being.

Self-Care and Boundaries

When it comes to your well-being, your personal boundaries are never more important. These measures are the best way to prioritize yourself and remind yourself that you are also important and that your needs and wants matter. When you have limitations safeguarding your self-care, you reduce the chances of neglecting to take care of yourself or make time to fulfill your needs.

Implementing Self-Care Practices Within Boundaries

Self-care is the act of growing and nurturing yourself. When it comes to setting boundaries with regard to your well-being, you'll learn that it's important to limit how much of your time and energy you're willing to dedicate to other people so that you have enough for yourself. Setting aside time for acts that nourish you will help you maintain your health, rest, and rejuvenate.

When you begin to set limits that cater to your self-care, you slowly begin to take back small pieces of yourself that you've been giving away. You can apply these measures to every area of your life and see the benefits. For example:

- Your emotional boundaries protect your peace and keep you from people who invalidate and disrespect you.
- Your mental boundaries release you from having to feel responsible for other people's feelings and experiences.
- Your physical boundaries safeguard your right to privacy and confidentiality.
- Your time boundaries prevent others from taking advantage of your kindness and protect you from overexhaustion and burnout.
- Your material boundaries allow you to keep your possessions safe and decide how you spend your money.

All of these areas where you previously had no boundaries become healthier once they're in place. You'll become more balanced and feel more whole overall. In the end, taking care of yourself first makes you better able to care for other people and more efficient at performing your job.

Overcoming Obstacles to Self-Care

With everything you likely have going on in your life, it's not surprising that you may find yourself faced with obstacles when it comes to practicing self-care. These hurdles might be internal, and they may take the form of feelings of guilt around taking time for yourself, or you may have placed unrealistically high expectations on yourself as to what self-care should entail. It could even be both. You might also be faced with external difficulties, like time constraints due to a demanding schedule and unavoidable social obligations, or you might still just be struggling to get the right life-work balance.

No matter what the nature of your challenges may be, there is always a solution. Don't allow these setbacks to become excuses as to why you can't practice self-care. Remind yourself that making time for your well-being is just as important as taking care of others or fulfilling your professional obligations.

Some strategies you might find helpful in overcoming these obstacles are:

- Setting realistic and achievable self-care goals for yourself. How you do it doesn't need to be perfect; it just needs to be effective. Little things add up over time.
- Scheduling self-care into your diary. This will force you to make it a priority. Treat it as you would any other appointment.
- Creating a self-care routine and then holding yourself accountable for sticking to it. Make it a habit and remember that consistency is vital.

Conclusion

In this chapter, we've acknowledged that setting boundaries in professional and digital areas can be difficult, but we've also seen that it's not impossible. We've discussed how boundaries at work will help your professional growth exponentially. You'll stop wasting hours on things that aren't important, and you'll no longer be constantly distracted by trivial matters. You'll protect yourself from being over-worked and taking on more than you can handle. And you'll create a more positive and productive work environment for yourself in which you can thrive. You'll be able to deliver your best in all your tasks because you'll be able to give all your focus to what you're doing. You'll also reduce your risk of burnout and increase your sense of job satisfaction.

In the digital world, you've seen that it's about curating your feed and taking control of what you put out there as well as what you expose yourself to. Creating healthy limits for yourself with regard to your internet consumption can have a great many benefits for your mental and emotional health. There's nothing wrong with using social media, but it's *how* you use it that will make all the difference.

Finally, we emphasized how important it is to never neglect self-care. You now know to make it both a habit and a priority by including it in your daily routine and trying your best to remain consistent with it. You may face some obsta-cles, but you will be able to overcome them with enough time and patience. Remember, self-care is the best way to ensure your continued overall health.

Now that we've overcome the hurdles of digital and profes-sional boundaries, it's time to bring it a little closer to home. In the next chapter, we'll be looking at boundaries in our relationships and how we can use them to guide our interac-tions with others.

Make a Difference with Your Review

"Kindness is a language which the deaf can hear and the blind can see."

— Mark Twain

Did you know that people who help others without expecting anything in return tend to live happier and more fulfilling lives? Well, that's exactly what I'm hoping we can achieve together.

Unlock the Power of Generosity

Now, I have a special request for you...

Would you be willing to help someone you've never met, without any recognition?

Imagine this person is just like you, or perhaps like you once were. They're seeking to improve their life, eager to make a difference, but unsure where to start.

Our goal is to make the principles of **Balanced Boundaries** accessible to everyone. Everything I do is driven by this mission. And the only way to achieve this is by reaching as many people as possible.

This is where your kindness comes into play. People often judge a book by its cover—and its reviews. So, on behalf of someone out there who's struggling to set healthy boundaries, I'm asking for your help:

Please leave a review for this book.

Your review won't cost you a dime and takes less than a minute, but it could change someone's life forever. Your words could help...

- ...one more person establish healthier relationships.
- ...one more individual find peace and balance.
- ...one more reader gain confidence and self-respect.
- ...one more soul start a journey of self-discovery.
- ...one more dream of personal growth come true.

To spread this kindness and make a real difference, all you need to do is leave a review. It's quick and easy:

If the thought of helping someone anonymously warms your heart, then you're exactly the kind of person I admire. Welcome to our community.

I'm thrilled to help you explore **Balanced Boundaries** in a way that's more impactful than you can imagine. You're going to love the insights and strategies in the upcoming chapters.

Thank you from the bottom of my heart. Now, let's get back to our journey together.

- Your biggest fan, S.H. Rhodes

P.S. - Fun fact: When you offer value to someone else, you become more valuable to them. If you think this book can help another soul and you'd like to spread some goodwill, consider sharing it with them.

6. Boundaries in Relationships

Emotional self-defense... When you set healthier relationship standards in your life, some people will take it personally. That's their issue, not yours. The distance isn't against them; it's for you. It's a boundary, not a grudge.

— Steve Maraboli

I once dated a girl during a phase of my life when I was exploring my sexuality. The relationship was fun and exciting, and we had a great time together during the years we spent as an item. However, I eventually came to the realization that perhaps it wasn't for me, and I decided to go back to dating men. This, of course, caused her deep hurt since it resulted in the ending of our relationship.

A few years passed, and we came back into each other's lives, but we never had a conversation clearly defining the nature of our relationship. This led to many lines being blurred. Were we simply having fun, or were we fulfilling a need in each other's lives during a time when we were both feeling lonely?

I'll admit, I was selfish in wanting both. As you can imagine, I ended up hurting her again, and in the process, I learned a crucial lesson about defining relationships.

When we fail to set clear boundaries within our relationships, we risk hurting both ourselves and those we care about. Being honest with someone will hurt them less than allowing them to live a lie or in a fantasy. If you want to foster healthy dynamics with the people in your life, you need to be able to set and communicate clear guidelines concerning the nature of your relationship and interactions and make sure you both have realistic expectations of each other.

In this chapter, to help put these considerations into practice, we'll be looking at this in more detail by delving into the concept of boundaries in the context of various relationships and exploring how the dynamics within those relationships can impact and affect your ability to communicate and enforce your needs and limits.

Setting Boundaries in Different Relationships

In this section, we'll be looking at how to set boundaries with romantic partners, with your family, and with your friends. As we do, you'll see that defining what is and isn't appropriate in different relationships is a unique process depending on the nature of your connection with the person you're setting the boundary with. Your dynamic can also adapt and change as you grow and develop or as you become more comfortable with someone. In that case, so will the way you define the relationship.

Boundaries in Romantic Relationships

Falling in love can be such a beautiful experience, but, if you want your relationship to last, you must establish healthy boundaries from the onset.

When you're falling for someone, it's normal to want to spend all of your time with them, and it's easy to let your whole life revolve around them. Despite what Hollywood has led you to believe, though, this isn't healthy. When you set boundaries with a partner, you prevent falling into a codependency. Limiting how much you share clearly defines where you end and where your partner begins. It's a way of protecting your personal identity within the relationship and ensuring that your needs and wants are being met.

In this context, boundaries are about communicating your preferences with your partner and drawing the parameters around where you feel the most comfortable and respected. It's about having the confidence to state your needs and trust that the person you're involved with will do their best to fulfill them. It's also about respecting your partner's needs and doing your best to fulfill them, too.

There are various facets within a romantic relationship in which boundaries are important:

Digital Boundaries

This relates to how comfortable you are with your partner posting about your relationship on social media and the pictures they share regarding the time you spend together. Some people choose not to make their romantic relationships public while others post every minute detail of their coupling. Deciding where each of you draws the line is an important conversation that you should have to prevent misunderstandings and conflicts in the future.

Digital boundaries also protect your right to privacy. This means that your partner has no right to demand your passwords or login information, and they shouldn't go through your phone without your permission.

Physical Boundaries

Physical boundaries within a romantic relationship can dictate how open you are with regard to displays of affection, either at home or in public spaces. Some people aren't entirely comfortable with kissing around others but are okay with holding hands, for example. Make sure you and your partner are both on the same page when it comes to where your physical comfort zones are.

Conflict within a relationship is normal, and it's to be expected that occasionally emotions may run high, and tempers may fly. However, it is never okay to resort to physical harm of any kind during a disagreement. A partner crossing this boundary is unforgivable, and if you find yourself in such a situation, you should do your best to remove yourself from it as soon as possible.

Financial Boundaries

Money is a very sensitive subject in most relationships. If you don't feel comfortable discussing your finances with your partner, you are under no obligation to. Things like how much you earn and how you spend money aren't their business unless you choose to share it with them or your finances are combined. If you live with them, it's important to discuss household expenses and how you will share them.

You should never feel pressured to give your significant other your banking or credit card information or to lend them money. Having said that, if you're comfortable being open about your finances with your partner and allowing them access to your accounts, that's also fine. As long as this is a decision you've come to on your own and not one you've felt pressured or manipulated into making. If you are married or know that the person you're with is who you want to spend your life with, then it is essential to be open and honest about money. Clear communication is essential if you want to build a healthy family as early as possible because it can take a long time to reach an agreement if both of you have your own spending habits and ways of managing money.

Emotional Boundaries

Having emotional boundaries with your partner means allowing yourself to determine how vulnerable you're comfortable being with them. You can decide how much of yourself you choose to expose in the relationship and how emotionally invested you're going to be. As the relationship deepens and your trust in your partner grows, these boundaries will also change.

Emotional boundaries are also important for preventing codependency. You need to be okay with being apart from your partner and should spend time nourishing your relationships with other people in your life. Independence is vital for creating a healthy dynamic.

Boundaries With Family

Setting boundaries with members of your family can be one of the most difficult tasks to undertake. This can be because they've probably gotten used to your relationship being a certain way for an extended period of time. Certain bad habits or unhealthy forms of communication are difficult to break. But remember what we've already said: Difficult doesn't mean impossible!

Putting limits in place with your parents can be even more difficult due to the imbalance of power. Depending on your cultural background, you might be restricted by cultural norms and expectations that require you to respect your elders. But this doesn't mean that you can't or shouldn't set boundaries with them. Respect is a two-way street, and you can communicate your boundaries while acknowledging their authority so that they may have a better reaction than if you tried to be too assertive or insistent.

Remind yourself that boundaries are not a way to damage or ruin your relationships but rather to enhance them and protect your mental and emotional peace. You will probably encounter some resistance, but that doesn't mean you should let it go. You are not responsible for other people's reactions to your needs, so don't let them guilt trip you or bully you into relenting.

Sometimes, your need for limits may lead to a rift, and you need to be okay with that. Nobody has a right to make your life miserable or disrespect you, no matter who they are. The hardest thing about standing up for yourself is enforcing consequences on those who fail to respect the lines you draw. Especially when those consequences result in the end of a relationship.

Boundaries in Friendships

Expressing how you want to be treated to your friends can feel awkward and uncomfortable. It's likely that you're afraid to hurt their feelings, or you're maybe afraid of losing their friendship. However, having clear boundaries with them will protect you from feeling like your relationships are all one-sided.

When you don't express your needs and desires, you can feel used and mistreated, which can lead to feelings of resentment. Communicating with your friends helps them understand how not to hurt you, make you feel disrespected, or put you in uncomfortable situations. It helps them understand how to treat and speak to you and what behavior is and isn't okay with you.

Maybe some of your friends are super playful and like to spank each other on the bum as a form of greeting. This might make you feel uncomfortable, but since nobody else in the friend group complains about it, you hold your tongue. Seemingly small boundary violations like this can eat away at the foundations of a friendship and cause it to deteriorate. For the sake of your well-being and to safeguard the longevity of your relationships, you need to be okay with communicating your discomfort in situations like this with the people around you so that they know to change their behavior.

Often, when we allow a behavior or pattern to continue over time, people will assume we're okay with it. For instance, if you're always the person who drives when you go out with your friends, they'll assume you enjoy being the designated driver. Even if you really wish one of them would volunteer for the role every now and then so that you can also enjoy a few drinks, they'll never know if you don't express this desire. As a result, you'll probably always end up being the designated driver, not because they're forcing it on you intentionally just to hurt you but because they assume you either don't mind or enjoy doing it.

This is just another example of how important it is for you to communicate with your friends. If you don't, you set a standard of behavior that they will continue to follow until you speak up and say something.

The Art of Communicating Boundaries

The ability to effectively communicate your boundaries is an essential skill to begin developing if you want your limits to be respected and understood. The power of boundaries is in setting them and implementing them within your relationships. That's the only way they'll be able to benefit you. As amazing as it is that you've come to understand what you want and need and why knowing these things is important, that knowledge won't do you any good without application.

Techniques for Clear and Empathetic Communication

The best way to ensure that your boundaries are respected is to make sure they're understood. When you express your needs with people, you must make sure they understand what you're asking for. It's also important for you to explain your limits in a way that doesn't make the person feel like you're attacking them or blaming them in any way. When you communicate empathetically, you make it easier for others to see things from your perspective and for you, in turn, to see things from theirs.

In communicating boundaries, remember to consider the following:

- You should know your needs and how you'd best like them to be met.
- You should understand your limitations and how you'd like them to be respected.
- Make sure you have a clear understanding of your boundaries. This will make it easier to communicate them with others.
- Be prepared for negative reactions and anticipate how you'll respond in those situations. Remember to never concede your boundaries for the sake of others.

- Have an open discussion around the conditions you're setting: It's a conversation, not a lecture. Allow others to respond and answer any questions they may have.
- Try to have a balance of assertiveness and empathy. Be willing to negotiate and be flexible for the sake of accommodating other peoples' boundaries.

So often, we only think of our boundaries after someone has crossed them, but you can avoid this by being proactive. Have a conversation early on in your relationships to make sure you're starting off on the right foot. And don't just leave it there. You can regularly rehash the conversation to make sure you're both still on the same page and are cognizant to continue respecting each other's boundaries.

Be as clear as possible when you're expressing yourself. Try not to give vague ideas of what you're asking for. Be specific, and you can even provide examples if that helps, as long as the scenarios you use aren't going to make the person you're addressing feel like you're attacking them or accusing them of anything.

You should also relay the consequences of violating your boundaries and what impact it will have on your relationship and future interactions. When people understand that they can't just walk all over you without facing repercussions, they're more likely to take you more seriously.

Responding to Boundary Violations

When people overstep your boundaries, you might not know how to respond. Other times, you might not even be aware that there has been a violation at all. Thankfully, there are signs you can look out for that will alert you to the fact that someone is either violating or disregarding your boundaries. Some of these signs are:

- a relationship beginning to display signs of codependency
- having to set the same boundary repeatedly
- a boundary being made fun of or you being made to feel ashamed of it
- being ignored after expressing that something is making you uncomfortable
- feeling uncomfortable around a certain person
- someone trying to manipulate you into changing your mind about a boundary

Dealing with violations can be tricky, as several factors will determine how best to handle the situation. What's paramount is that you address it promptly, right as it happens. Allowing too much time to lapse before you say something will make your response less impactful. Saying something at the moment will also make it easier for the person to immediately understand where they've gone wrong and to change their behavior in the moment. It will also save you from having to hold onto the emotion the violation sparked, and you won't build up resentment and feelings of frustration at their behavior. Just rip it off like a bandaid and get it over with so that you can both learn from the experience and move on.

There are other factors to consider when responding to someone crossing a line, such as the nature of your relationship with the person who's done it. Obviously, you can't react the same way with your boss as you would with a close friend who overstepped in the same way. It's important to take the power dynamics within the relationship as well as the level of closeness you have with the person into consideration when formulating your response.

Ask yourself if you think the person is willing to change their behavior, determine if they've overstepped by mistake or if they simply don't respect you, and also consider how long they've been repeating the violation. You should also take how firm the boundary is into account. Not all of them are the same. Some can be seen merely as preferences while others are completely nonnegotiable. This will also play a factor in how you address the situation and what consequences you choose to enforce.

Look at the impact the violation has on you. Is it just something that's annoying, or does it cause you serious distress? Ask yourself if you've set clear and consistent limits. Sometimes when we're haphazard with maintaining our boundaries, people begin to see them as optional. Once you've thought about all of these variables, you'll be better equipped to address the situation.

Now that you've reflected on the violation, here are some ideas on what you can do about it:

- Keep reinforcing your boundaries and stand your ground. I know this isn't always easy, but the only way people will respect your boundaries is if you consistently stick to them, no matter what.

- Keep track of violations and regularly reassess them. Sometimes, you'll find that you haven't been as consistent with enforcing boundaries as you should have been, which has led to repeated issues. If you find that you have kept the line in place, but the person in question has continued to cross it, you need to decide if you're willing to continue to accept that.

- Don't move the goalposts. Be very clear with yourself about what you will and will not tolerate. You may find that your boundaries recede over time, and you slowly begin to accept a little more than you did before. When you have a very clear picture in your mind of where you draw the line, you can prevent this from happening.

- Make peace with the fact that some people will never respect your boundaries, no matter what you do. This can be a bitter pill to swallow at first, but you'll save yourself a lot of unnecessary stress and anxiety in the long run.

- Consider your other options. You have every right to limit or cut contact with someone who continues to disrespect you.

Relationship Growth Through Boundaries

Healthy boundaries form the foundation of a healthy relationship in which both parties grow as individuals and thrive as a couple. When your relationships lack them, you may become too enmeshed with your partners. Without the solid guidance of these safeguards, it will become hard for you to remember where you end and where the other person begins. You can end up losing yourself in your relationship, becoming a watered-down version of the person you were before. You may end up changing things about yourself to make the other person happy and sacrificing things you once enjoyed in favor of their interests.

Using Boundaries to Foster Healthy Relationships

Boundaries play an essential role in creating a nurturing environment within your relationships. When you have healthy communication in your relationships, you produce an atmosphere of mutual respect where both you and the other person involved understand and honor one another's limits. This leads to dynamics where you are considerate of each other and treat each other as equals.

It also protects your identity. You're better able to maintain your autonomy and pursue your personal interests within the relationship, as well as express your desires openly and without fear. This independence will cultivate self-improvement and personal growth for both of you.

When you set clear boundaries within your relationships, you prevent misunderstandings and reduce conflicts. This is because you and the other person both have a deep awareness of one another's needs and expectations. You're comfortable communicating openly and honestly about your desires, and this creates an opportunity for healthy interactions.

Boundaries help create a safe space for you within your relationship, where you feel like your emotional well-being is being nourished and respected. When you set them with your partner, you protect yourself from feeling unappreciated, used, or mistreated, and instead, you feel supported and validated.

Relationships that are built on a respect for both parties' needs and desires are a great catalyst for personal growth. You learn to express yourself, set your limits and expectations, and have them respected and validated in return. This will create a stronger bond with your partner and improve your relationship as a whole.

Balancing Independence and Interdependence

Finding the right harmony between independence and interdependence in your relationship can be a delicate balancing act that takes a lot of time and effort to get right. The ultimate goal is for you to be able to thrive both as a couple and as individuals. This means that you need to dedicate as much time to growing and improving your relationship as you do to growing and improving yourselves. It might sound impossible, but the secret ingredient is having the right boundaries.

One of the most important things to stay vigilant of when you enter a new relationship is maintaining your sense of self. We can easily get into relationships to escape loneliness or to fill some sort of void. Approaching a relationship with this attitude is unhealthy and can lead to codependence. Knowing who you are without a partner so that you don't lose yourself in your relationships is imperative. It means having a strong set of values, being aware of what you like, spending time with friends and family, and continuing to pursue your personal interests outside of the relationship.

If you're wondering what a healthy, independent relationship looks like, here are a few key traits it will have:

- active listening
- clear communication
- accountability for both parties' actions and behavior
- a safe space in which you can be vulnerable
- comfort in approaching your partner about issues
- quality time together as a priority
- time to pursue individual interests
- self-care practice

Boundaries in Conflict Resolution and Harmony

Some people can't stand it when you raise your voice or wave your arms at them when you're upset. Others become passionate during emotionally fueled arguments, and this is simply how they express themselves.

When conflict arises within the relationship, boundaries are what will help you create the framework in which you can address the issue in a constructive manner. When problems arise, the boundaries you've set with each other will guide you to know what your partner's limits are with regard to acceptable behavior. Knowing this will enable you to best understand how to effectively communicate with them during conflicts without upsetting or offending them and escalating the situation.

Conclusion

By now, you should be fairly comfortable with the concept of boundaries, and you should feel confident in your ability to communicate them effectively in various relationships. Next, we're going to be digging a little deeper and exploring some of the more complex issues you may face when it comes to expressing what you want and need in relationships. Forewarned is forearmed, as they say. The surer you are of your boundary-setting skills, the easier it will be for you to stick to them and maintain them in difficult circumstances.

7. Advanced Topics in Boundary Setting

Walls keep everybody out. Boundaries teach them where the door is.

— Mark Groves

I had a coworker once who came across as aloof and unapproachable. She kept her distance from people, and I had the sense that she was someone who was reluctant to let others in.

At first, I found her attitude rather odd and assumed she had a disagreeable personality. When colleagues asked her questions, she was evasive or would simply state that she didn't wish to discuss certain things about herself and her personal life. I thought that sharing more about myself would encourage her to let her guard down and reciprocate. However, I hoped in vain. She stood her ground, maintained strong boundaries, and kept our interactions strictly professional.

I was quite taken aback by her behavior. I thought it was strange that someone would be so determined not to share anything about themselves. After all, everyone else did it and thought nothing of it! Why couldn't she just interact with me as she would with a friend?

As time went on, I began to appreciate and even admire her demeanor with her colleagues. It wasn't that she didn't interact with them at all; she was very friendly and polite. She simply had firm professional limits with the people at the office. Once I'd gotten used to the way she was, I learned to respect her privacy, and I noticed that other coworkers did as well.

From this experience, I learned how important it is to not immediately make assumptions about a person who comes across as different. Instead, there was a lot that she could teach me, and I learned that I could probably use a few more boundaries in my professional life.

I'm sure we've all had a similar experience with a coworker at some point in our lives. I hope you can see that situation with fresh eyes and come to appreciate a strong display of professional boundaries when you see it!

In this chapter, we'll be exploring boundaries in more specific and unusual contexts, such as intricate social settings, and we'll discuss your public persona. This chapter will also address how it isn't always easy to know how to keep strong boundaries in certain scenarios. We'll also how, much like my coworker, you may come across as strange to others at first. However, with time and perseverance, people can learn to understand, accept, and respect the boundaries that you set.

Unique Boundary Challenges

At this point, you might have a decent grasp on your personal boundaries and how to set them, but what happens when you're put in a different situation or context? Or when the measures you've had in place are outdated for where you currently are in your life? Let's explore some of the unique situations that may present themselves to you in life and how you can adapt to suit them.

Navigating Boundaries in Diverse Social Settings

As you know, boundaries are not universal. The way you communicate and express them in one situation might be completely inappropriate in another. One of the stumbling blocks you might run into is when you're interacting with a diverse group of people who may not have the same understanding of what is and isn't appropriate as you. In these situations, it's important to adjust your expectations to respect your differences and make your communication more effective. When you're dealing with a mix of people of different cultures and beliefs, it's important to come into the space with an attitude of respect, compassion, and awareness of those differences.

As we've mentioned in earlier chapters, cultures will greatly influence approaches to relationships. Things like the way people communicate and approach personal space may vary, depending on where they're from and what they've been exposed to. If you're unsure of another person's under-standing of what is and isn't appropriate in interactions and how best to relate to them, there's nothing wrong with asking! For example, if you're meeting someone for the first time, ask them if they'd prefer a hug or a handshake. When you openly express a desire to cater to their customs, you open the door to a more harmonious exchange than if you just assume.

Being open-minded and empathetic are also great ways to learn more about other people's customs and beliefs, as well as to share your own. You don't have to agree with someone to respect their boundaries. By showing mutual respect, you will be in a better position to gain insight into new ways of doing things and new ideas.

Adjusting Boundaries in Major Life Transitions

As we go through life, we change and grow, and it's impor-tant that your current set of boundaries always reflects where you are and what you need. The same safeguards that are holding you together today might be the ones holding you back tomorrow. For this reason, it's advisable that you consistently evaluate where you draw a line, ensuring that it's still serving its intended purpose.

Let's look at some helpful ways to adapt your boundaries as you transition through life:

- Reflect on your current boundaries and ask yourself if they're still relevant and affirming to your present needs and expectations.

- Re-evaluate your boundaries. Assess if they align with your current needs, or if you can adjust them to match where you are now.
- Don't forget to communicate with the people around you, whether that means renegotiating a previously set boundary or simply clarifying one that seems to have fallen by the wayside.
- Keep self-care as a priority. Especially during times of change, you need to remember not to neglect yourself.
- Stay flexible. Transitions can be stressful and unpredictable. You may find yourself needing to compromise a lot more than you're used to in order to make the process smoother.

Maintaining what you do and don't tolerate during a transitional time in your life can be difficult, especially with so many other things going on. However, you may find that standing your ground during these times will bring you a sense of comfort and contribute positively to your overall well-being.

Addressing Unusual or Sensitive Boundary Situations

You might find yourself in a particularly tricky situation where you're not sure how to handle yourself. In these cases, communicating how you want to be treated might seem like a mammoth task, and you may be tempted to just turn a blind eye. However, learning how to maintain your boundaries, even in awkward or unusual situations, will grow your confidence in setting them and make it easier for you to continue to implement them in all other aspects of your life.

Practicing active listening and empathy can go a long way to easing some of your initial discomfort and give you a better understanding of how best to address it. When you allow for open and honest communication without judgment, you make room for mutual respect and give yourself an opportunity to understand different perspectives. Remember to communicate your boundaries assertively and don't be afraid to say no. You can validate others' feelings and perspectives and still effectively explain your point without causing conflict or discomfort.

In an unusual scenario, you might need to think outside of the box and find a more creative problem-solving approach to assert yourself. Just remember to stay calm and don't be afraid to ask for help or advice if you feel like you need it.

Boundaries in Special Contexts

Boundaries can exist in any dynamic, even those where you can't immediately see a place for them. Below, we'll look at some of the more uncommon scenarios you might need to set them in and how you can best go about doing so.

Exploring Boundaries in Unconventional Relationships

With the internet becoming more accessible, there has been an increase in the number and types of unconventional relationships you'll see in today's world. For example, are you in a long-distance relationship? Do you know someone with a considerable age gap in their relationship? Maybe you've heard of someone who has a living-apart-together relationship, meaning they've decided to live separately for reasons such as work, family, or their children's education.

You may think that people who are engaged in open marriages, polyamorous relationships, or any other nontraditional form of romantic engagement don't have many boundaries. On the contrary, clear limits are probably the biggest factor in the success of these relationships. Boundaries set the benchmark for each member and ensure that all of their personal needs, desires, and expectations are in alignment.

These relationships face societal scrutiny and internal conflicts, so those within them must be able to deal with issues effectively for the relationship to succeed. This requires a great deal of resilience and understanding. Open communication is as important here as it is in any other relationship. Each person involved must feel safe and comfortable enough with their partners to honestly express their needs, expectations, and limits, and they need to feel that they will be taken into consideration and respected.

Clear communication of needs and desires is the foundation upon which trust is built in unconventional relationships. Having firm boundaries within them will limit jealousy and help define clear parameters for each member. Without them, these relationships will crumble.

Long-Distance Relationships

My husband and I started a long-distance relationship that lasted for six years before we could regularly see each other in person and eventually live together. During those years, it felt like we had plenty of freedom. However, a foundation of trust, as well as many boundaries and expectations were set and implemented between us, which helped us successfully navigate through the hard times.

Having a successful long-distance relationship requires a lot of open communication, trust, and, of course, boundaries. Having these measures in place are vital for ensuring that each partner feels safe within the relationship and feels that their needs are being met and respected. This involves communicating your expectations with your partner regarding things like emotional support, how often you'd like to be in contact, and the possibility of virtual intimacy.

Regularly check in with your partner regarding the dynamics of your relationship and how you can improve or adjust the boundaries you've set both for yourselves and each other. These relationships require honesty to navigate and make them work. Don't be too afraid to express it if something is making you uncomfortable or to address a situation that you feel has crossed one of your boundaries. The only way to prevent conflicts and misunderstandings, which will cause strain on a relationship that's already under the pressure of distance, is to communicate frequently and honestly with your partner.

Setting Boundaries in High-Stress or High-Stakes Environments

When you're working in an environment where you feel stressed or pressured to perform your best, boundaries can be a crucial component for protecting your mental health and emotional well-being. When you feel like there's a lot at stake, you're may often be tempted to push yourself beyond your limits or resort to people-pleasing behaviors to prove yourself. These sacrifices may not have the desired effect and may inevitably reduce your effectiveness or result in burnout.

Having limits in place in these scenarios is about more than just safeguarding your well-being. It can also reduce stress levels of everyone else involved. When everyone knows what's expected of them and what each person's limits are, they will feel a lot more at ease completing their tasks. Make sure you communicate your own limits clearly and never be afraid to say no, even if it means disappointing someone. Your health and well-being need to be your top priority.

Boundaries in Public Life and Online Personas

Setting boundaries in public spaces and in your online interactions is an essential part of maintaining your mental health and also your privacy. These limits dictate both how you interact with others as well as how you portray yourself. They also limit how much personal information you share with others publicly and how much access people have to you.

Some good examples of setting boundaries in these areas are:

- Allowing yourself to place limits on what you're comfortable with. Whether that's about accepting friend requests on Facebook or not sharing intimate details of your personal life with people you barely know.

- Curate your circle. Be discerning with who you allow to follow you on social media and think twice about everything you post.
- Find the balance between being open and keeping yourself safe. Be careful about how much information about yourself you share online.
- Online relationships have a tendency to move at hyperspeed so make sure you pace yourself. Get to know the person before committing to anything and make sure they really are who they say they are.
- Think of your reputation. Remember that the internet is forever, and what you post on there will probably be available in some form for a long time.

The Future of Boundaries

Looking forward, how will our boundaries change and develop in the future? How does the influence of technology and the continuation of globalization impact the way people understand and form personal boundaries? Let's explore some of these ideas and how we can anticipate incorporating them moving forward.

The Role of Technology and Globalization in Shaping Boundaries

With technology advancing the way it has been over the last few decades, the world really isn't as big as it once used to be. The internet has made it easier for us to interact with people from all walks of life and be exposed to others from many different cultures around the world. As a result, our knowledge has expanded exponentially. At the touch of a button, we can gain intimate knowledge about customs and countries that we never would have had the ability to learn about or explore before.

Now, people from all over the world can share their ideas and experiences, which has a big influence on our perspectives and understanding. This global knowledge makes it easier to interact with people from diverse cultural backgrounds. The interconnectedness that the internet affords us has also given us the opportunity to cast a wider net socially. We can now virtually meet with people from anywhere in the world and form connections with them, even if we've never met. As a result, we can expand our own opinions and beliefs based on these shared experiences.

Setting Boundaries as an Evolving Practice in a Changing World

Boundaries are not fixed points, and we've already explored how you need to learn how to adapt them during major life transitions. But this isn't the only factor that you need to consider. As much as you need to adjust your approach to reflect how your life changes, you should also adjust what you do or don't tolerate to suit how the world is changing.

We've just discussed the effects of technology and globalization on our ability to understand and connect with the world, and this will continue to have an impact and influence on our personal boundaries. The things we see as nonnegotiable now may not be that way in the future. For example, when they were growing up, your parents were probably taught to never get in a car with a stranger, and yet, these days, we don't think twice before ordering an Uber!

While certain principles are cast in stone when it comes to our personal set of values and beliefs, others should be flexible. If you want to grow and evolve and not be left behind as the world changes, you need to practice flexibility.

Conclusion

At this point in this book, you are on your way to becoming a boundary master! You're clued up on the basics and have learned how to adjust to changing circumstances and adapt to unusual scenarios. Your newfound ability to express your needs and limitations in diverse social settings and high-stress environments has probably given you a big boost in confidence.

However, you've also seen that sometimes the rules don't apply. As much as you can master the basics and tweak them when required, you may find yourself in a situation where none of what you've learned so far applies. In those situations, you need to learn how to think outside of the box and come up with unique and creative techniques for setting boundaries. We'll be exploring this further in the next chapter.

8. Specialized Techniques in Boundary Management

Boundaries represent awareness, knowing what the limits are, and then respecting those limits.

— David W. Earle

You may likely have seen or heard someone make a comment to the effect of "Oh, that's so nice of him," in response to someone, or yourself, performing a selfless act, such as volunteering.

This behavior is often seen as exemplary, yet, as you may know, people can slowly begin to take advantage of that kindness over time. If for some reason you were to stop being so generous, the same people may all judge and condemn you, and you'll find yourself suddenly being put in a position where you need to explain yourself, as if your generosity is something that is owed. On the other hand, someone else who rarely gives back might hail even greater praise and acknowledgment for their generosity than you, a person who gives so often and so selflessly of yourself.

I have found myself in similar positions on many occasions. That is not to say that my generosity has ever been for show or praise and acknowledgment. I give freely because it's something I genuinely enjoy doing. But how are we to set boundaries or limitations on traits such as kindness, things that are just a part of who we are? And how do we protect ourselves from being judged and vilified by others? The answer is that we can't. This is why your boundaries are for nobody but yourself.

To avoid feeling unappreciated or taken advantage of, it is important that you establish clear expectations, even in the situations just described. You might want to clarify that your willingness to volunteer is not without limitations and that you are able to do so only in accordance with your availability or within your means. It would be best if you made it clear that you also have other priorities and responsibilities that require your time and attention.

If you do find yourself feeling taken for granted, you're well within your rights to take a step back to re-evaluate your involvement. Always remember the important role that boundaries play in safeguarding your well-being. You should never put yourself in a situation where you're giving at the expense of your health and happiness.

That being said, it's impossible to completely disregard the expectations that others place on us, particularly when they're expressed by a great number of people and feel unfeasible. To suggest that you simply ignore them would be misleading, and I'm aiming to provide you with practical guidance in this book. To that end, I will only share realistic strategies that you can use to help you overcome the feelings of guilt associated with letting people down in favor of your self-interest and self-preservation.

Learning how to handle and cope with criticism is a part of the journey. As long as you have set clear limits for yourself and have honored your principles, you don't need to worry about other people's opinions. At the end of the day, you will never be able to please everyone, so you shouldn't feel bad about saying no when you need to.

Setting boundaries is not about giving less or being less generous or kind. It's about taking care of yourself and ensuring that what you do give is both sustainable and appreciated.

Now that we have that understanding in place, we can navigate the rest of this chapter, in which we will be delving into the ethics and morals behind setting boundaries and where you need to draw the line. We'll also be getting into some of the more complex situations in which you may find yourself needing to stand your ground and exploring a few creative and unconventional methods you can use to do this.

Innovative Approaches to Setting Boundaries

So far, we've explored the best strategies and formulas you can use to help you create your personal boundaries. You've looked into yourself and gained self-awareness of your values, needs, and wants and learned ways to express them through effective communication. But that doesn't mean you need to be so rigid and clinical in your approach. Your method of setting boundaries can be as unique as your boundaries are. You can also tap into your creative side to help you build and maintain them! Let's look at some different strategies you can try to help you on your boundary-setting journey.

Exploring Creative and Unconventional Methods

Some people are more visually stimulated and might not find the idea of sitting down and writing lists appealing. But that doesn't mean you can't get the most out of the process of creating boundaries—it just means you need to think a little outside the box! Let's explore some of the more artistic ways you can use for this.

Boundary Symbols

Having a tangible symbol can serve as a constant reminder of your principles and their importance to you. Find a few objects that you can use as a physical representation of your values, needs, and wants. It can be gemstones, jewelry, a specific type of flower, or anything that holds a special meaning to you. Try and place the items around your house or in places where you can see them often so that they serve as a constant reminder of what they represent. Whenever you see or wear this object, let it be a reminder to you of your boundaries.

Boundary Rituals

Incorporate your boundaries into your daily routine. Create a ritual for yourself that you can perform twice a day, once in the morning and once in the evening. As you begin your day, include a kind of boundary-setting practice. This can be repeating affirmations, meditating, or journaling and writing down your boundaries. This will help you go into your day with a clear picture of the lines you need to draw and the limits you need to reinforce.

At the end of your day, take some time for reflection. Think about how effectively you managed to enforce your boundaries and identify any situations you could have improved on communicating them. Including this in your daily routine will help make the actions surrounding them more of a habit and an integral part of your life and interactions.

Boundary Playlist

Sometimes, music can give you the emotional upliftment that you need to take action. Having a playlist that gets you going can help you when you just need a minute to yourself to remember to stick to your guns and make your boundaries a priority.

Create a playlist of songs that make you feel empowered and reflect the vision you have for how you want to conduct yourself and your relationships. Make sure the lyrics of the songs are relevant to the desired effect you'd like the boundaries you've created to have on your life. Listen to it whenever you feel that you need a little more motivation to stay persistent.

Boundary Vision Board

Create a vision board that visually represents your boundaries. Fill it with images and words that you feel best depict the measures you'd like to implement and that motivate or inspire you to pursue them. Use inspiring and uplifting images and words that help you visualize the life you can have if you successfully incorporate your boundaries. Also include those that represent your limits so that you can keep them at the forefront of your mind.

Hang your vision board in a place where you will see it often, and, whenever you look at it, take a moment to reflect on the elements and what they mean to you. This will help you consistently reinforce your desires in your mind and keep you motivated to actively pursue implementing the necessary measures in your life.

Integrating Technology and Digital Tools in Boundary Management

Living in a digital age has its advantages. There are many tools you can use to help you along your journey. For those of us whose jobs require us to constantly be on our phones, using apps and technology to help is a great way to incorporate setting boundaries into your life more seamlessly. So, let's look at several apps you can use to enhance your experience:

Well-Being Tracking Apps

If you're looking for something that will help you identify your needs and values as well as figure out where your limits are, you should consider downloading a comprehensive health-tracking app. They allow you to identify situations that cause you anxiety or anger or that cause you to be overwhelmed. These feelings are normally present in areas of your life where you lack boundaries. By using these apps to help you identify those areas, you'll be better equipped to know what boundaries you need to set and where.

Mind-Mapping Apps

After identifying where you need to set your boundaries, you need to reflect on how you're going to start implementing the changes. A great way to do this is to brainstorm some ideas using a mind-mapping app. You can outline what measures you need to enforce and figure out practical strategies you can try that will work for you. Having a visual representation that you can manipulate and move around will make it easier for you to navigate different ways of having your needs realized.

Mindfulness Journal App

The only way to assess the effectiveness of your boundaries and keep an eye on your progress is for you to document it, and a journaling app is a great way for you to do this on the go. You can quickly make note of things as they unfold and return to assess the overall success of your day in the evening. Having a journal will also give you a chance to explore how you feel about where your journey is taking you, and you'll also be able to look back on situations that may have arisen in the past, making it easier for you to spot patterns and identify possible triggers.

Boundaries in Complex Situations

When you're placed in an unfamiliar, uncertain, or uncomfortable situation, sometimes your boundaries are the only thing that make you feel safe. When you know what your limitations are and are confident in how you've expressed them, you are more easily able to endure difficult situations. Let's look at how you can apply this in some of the more difficult situations you may find yourself in.

Strategies for Difficult or Sensitive Scenarios

You're not going to get along with everyone you meet in life. That's just a given. At some point or another, you will come into contact with people who you just can't see eye to eye with, and that's okay. However, there's a difference between simply not being able to get along with someone and handling difficult personalities. These people don't seem to get along with anyone and can make any situation immediately uncomfortable and unbearable for everyone involved. Establishing limits with them can be a challenge, but it is unavoidable if you'd like to preserve your own mental and emotional well-being.

If you're unsure how to recognize a difficult person, here are three common characteristics they have that you can look out for:

- Difficult people often show behavioral patterns and traits that manifest in the form of inconsistency, resentment, dominance, and manipulation.
- Such people are often emotionally draining to anyone who has to deal with them. If you find yourself consistently feeling depleted after interacting with someone, you may be dealing with a difficult person.
- They often repeat the same cycle of conflict and tension. Being able to spot these patterns in their

interactions with you or others can be a good
indicator that this is a person to avoid.

Setting boundaries with difficult people isn't easy because
you're almost certainly going to get pushback. Still, for the
sake of your sanity, it's important that you put them in place.
Some helpful strategies you can use to do this are:

- Express to them what you are going to do but don't
  attempt to tell them what to do because that won't go
  well. Remember, you're only in control of your own
  decisions and actions. You have no control over
  other people. However, in stating what your
  intentions are, you can limit their options.
- Bring up the concept of boundaries at a time when
  you're both calm and not in the middle of a heated
  discussion. State your point in a firm but otherwise
  unemotional tone and keep the conversation as
  relaxed and neutral as possible.
- Keep the discussion centered around yourself, what
  your limits are, and what you're willing and able to
  do. Don't attempt to suggest what they should do or
  guess how they might be feeling. When you keep the
  conversation about your boundaries, you reduce the
  opportunities for them to argue.
- Acknowledge that you could also be mistaken. When
  you make it clear that the measures you're putting in
  place are simply based upon your own opinion,
  limits, and experiences, you create a space where
  they don't feel like anything is being dictated to or
  imposed upon them.

Balancing Boundaries in Power Dynamics and Hierarchical Structures

When it comes to contexts in which there's an unequal distribution of power within a relationship or a social hierarchy at play, having and maintaining your personal boundaries is crucial. The biggest challenge you'll face in these situations is fear of repercussions or social pressure.

You won't always want to express your personal boundaries with someone who's in a position of authority over you because you're afraid of jeopardizing your job, losing favor, and maybe suffering long-term consequences in your career as a result. In hierarchies, you may experience a sense of obligation that will cause feelings of guilt whenever the idea of boundaries comes up.

When you're asserting yourself with people in positions of authority, you can still be polite and respectful without sacrificing your well-being. Remember to make your limits clear so that you don't overextend yourself or take on more than you can realistically handle. You have a right to clearly define your limits and not be pressured or coerced into accepting behavior and treatment that makes you feel uncomfortable, not even from your superiors.

The Ethics of Setting Boundaries

The ethics of setting boundaries is a complex and delicate concept. When we think of ethics in this regard, we need to consider the aspects of personal autonomy, interpersonal dynamics, and societal norms. Taking these three key factors into consideration will help us navigate the best course of action in many scenarios.

Personal autonomy refers to each person's inherent right to set personal boundaries for the sake of protecting their own well-being and preserving their self-respect. However, ethically, it's also important to take the autonomy of others into account when we're asserting our needs and expectations. Let's delve further into the concept of ethics in this context.

Navigating Moral and Ethical Considerations

Having a strong sense of what you will or will not accept is the foundation of making ethical decisions when it comes to setting boundaries. Without these considerations, you might fall prey to people who use unethical tactics such as emotional or psychological manipulation against you.

In the workplace, having these measures in place means avoiding exploitation, treating all of your subordinates and colleagues fairly, and ensuring the well-being of all your employees. In your personal relationships, it means striking the right balance between emotional availability and self-care.

When you set boundaries ethically, you communicate your limits in such a way that they don't cause harm to others. You don't force your boundaries on others as demands, and you don't resort to tactics like manipulation to get what you want. You show consideration for others' rights to have boundaries and respect the outcomes of their decisions.

The Role of Empathy and Compassion in Boundary Decisions

When you set boundaries with empathy, you give thought to how your boundaries will affect and impact others. Being sensitive to others is what aids you in acknowledging their needs and their right to have them as well as doing the same for yourself. Compassion extends even further beyond that: It gives you the desire to help others improve their well-being and alleviate any source of discomfort they may be experiencing.

Communicating your needs, desires, and tolerances with consideration helps you remember that these safeguards are never about alienating yourself from others but about being able to protect your well-being while also doing what you can to take care of others.

Respecting Others' Boundaries While Upholding Your Own

Sometimes, it might feel like you're struggling to find the balance between assertively reinforcing your boundaries while also accommodating the preferences of others. Being able to uphold your boundaries while still validating other people's right to have their own is based on mutual respect and understanding.

Compromise is a great strategy to use in these situations. Try to find common ground with the other person and remember to be flexible when it comes to working toward a win-win situation. It isn't always about one person getting what they want and the other having to make a sacrifice. Find a way that you can both feel happy and comfortable with the outcome.

Be empathetic and be open to seeing things from the other person's perspective. Put yourself in their shoes and consider their needs and feelings. Allow yourself to prioritize boundaries that are completely nonnegotiable but also be willing to adjust others that aren't.

Communicate assertively but be kind and compassionate with your words. Don't invalidate the feelings and experiences of others. Rather, listen to what they have to say and respect their boundaries just as you'd like them to respect yours.

Conclusion

Now that we've reached the conclusion of this chapter, you know that creating and setting boundaries isn't an exact science. It's about finding ways to navigate even the most difficult situations with calmness and confidence and being able to show empathy and understanding to those around you. Being respectful to those in authority doesn't mean catering to their every whim. Even in stressful and high-stakes scenarios, you can still set your personal limits without guilt or fear.

You've also seen that having boundaries doesn't mean forcing them onto people as if they're demands. You can avoid this by approaching standing your ground from an ethical and compassionate point of view. Respect the autonomy of others and recognize their right to have their own boundaries and needs. You can uphold yours while still respecting those of others. All it takes is a little bit of compromise and a lot of empathy and compassion.

Moving forward, we will explore how boundaries encompass every aspect of our lives, not just the direct relationships we have in our professional and personal lives. In the next chapter, we'll be exploring the topic of boundaries as they relate to our culture and our wider social circles and communities as a whole.

9. Boundaries and Community

Your personal boundaries protect the inner core of your identity and your right to choices.

— Gerard Manley Hopkins

I used to be a people pleaser, someone who would agree to everything for the sake of peace and avoiding conflict. I've found that most people who grew up in my Asian culture are the same.

I recall many instances following a work meeting where my manager would ask me why I hadn't expressed my opinion and why I'd remained silent. I realize now that this was due to me feeling like I didn't have my own voice. At that point, I felt that my inexperience coupled with being a recent immigrant meant my opinions weren't valid. I thought I didn't know enough to be able to express my thoughts.

However, my views have since changed. I can see now how, in coming from a different cultural background, my opinion would actually have been and would continue to be a valuable asset in these conversations. Being able to offer a different perspective and provide an outside opinion and feedback is an incredible catalyst for creativity and new ideas!

Something I've noticed regarding people from my native country in Asia is how apologetic we are. We say "sorry" or "excuse me" excessively and very rarely respond with an outright no even when we should or want to. We beat around the bush in an attempt to use more subtle or tactful methods of communicating our dissent, which only leads to ineffective communication and misunderstandings when the people we're speaking to fail to grasp what we're trying to say. We hardly ever express our disagreement straightforwardly.

I personally believe that the overly apologetic nature of our communication is an attempt to smooth things over and avoid damaging our relationships. Since moving to America, I've learned that most people see this as a sign of weakness or guilt, and they prefer to avoid it. This has been a great lesson for me in the way I communicate. I honestly feel that most Americans are far more assertive than those of us from Asian countries.

As you may have guessed from this introduction, in this chapter, we'll be exploring how cultural differences manifest in the formation of boundaries. We'll look at how our cultural beliefs, education, and upbringing help form our ideas around relationships and interactions and how societal structures influence our ability to set and maintain boundaries.

Boundaries in Social Groups and Communities

It can become so easy to lose yourself in the crowd when it comes to being a part of a bigger whole. You can begin to identify so much with a group's identity that you completely forget your own. Having boundaries is what will allow you to be yourself, no matter where you are or who you're with.

The Role of Boundaries in Group Dynamics

Personal boundaries in the context of a group helps everyone involved maintain their sense of respect and well-being, and they make co-operation easier. When working with several other people, it's important for you to be aware of your limits and express them clearly to the other members of the group. Communicate your limits clearly and assertively but also respect and be open to accommodating the boundaries of others as well.

When you set boundaries within a group, you help ensure that everyone involved feels safe and respected. Knowing where each other's boundaries and limitations are makes it easier to communicate more effectively and ensures that interactions are more productive. It also fosters a spirit of mutual respect, whereby you teach others how to treat you and learn how they'd like to be treated in return.

Navigating Cultural and Social Norms

We live in a diverse world filled with a variety of different cultures. As such, it's not realistic to expect everyone we meet to share the same set of values and beliefs we do. Understanding how to set boundaries in these contexts can be tricky, but with a little sensitivity and open-mindedness, you will surely find your way.

Here are some tips on how to approach setting boundaries with an inclusive mindset:

Do Your Research

Go online and read up about different cultures and their customs. Put yourself in social situations where you'll be exposed to people from various backgrounds and ask them about their values and experiences. The more you learn about other people, the easier it will be to see their perspectives, making communication easier and more effective.

Be Curious

Whenever you come across someone who hasn't had the same upbringing as you or who comes from a different country, see it as an opportunity to learn. Ask them about their traditions and beliefs. By watching them closely you'll be able to pick up differences in the way they communicate using nonverbal gestures and body language. And don't be afraid to ask questions. The more you know, the better equipped you'll be to interact with them in the future.

Be Open-Minded

Try not to judge people based on your past experiences and be open to re-evaluating your beliefs and opinions. Show respect for their cultures, beliefs, and values, even if they're very different from your own. Sometimes, when you listen to a different perspective with an open mind, you end up realizing that your mindset has shifted. The more you learn, the more informed you can be about your opinions and thoughts.

Community Influences on Setting Personal Boundaries

The community in which you live and grew up plays an important role in influencing your ability or willingness to set personal boundaries. Different cultures have different ideas of what personal space and privacy mean, and they also have unique rules regarding what is considered acceptable behavior.

In some cultures, like mine, direct confrontation and expression of needs or limits is generally frowned upon. This makes assertive communication difficult, as it may cause offense. When you're living in a tight-knit community, the social pressure you feel to be a certain way can make it extremely uncomfortable to try to communicate how you want to be treated. Peer pressure and fear of rejection and isolation might cause you to just want to go with the flow and accept things as they are, even if you're unhappy and feel that you are being disrespected.

Being subject to family traditions and having shared values passed down from generation to generation also means that voicing how you would like to be treated can be seen as an insult. Trying to break free from expectations and imposed values and beliefs is an extremely difficult task, and that's probably why so few people do it in the end. For many, the risk is not worth the reward.

Boundary Advocacy and Education

Imagine a society where everyone upheld and respected each other's boundaries! As much as this might seem like a fantasy, we can play a small role in making it a reality, at least in our own lives and the lives of those around us.

The first step is to get involved in educating others about boundaries and advocating for them in our communities. You'd be surprised how many people know very little about how barriers and safeguards to our well-being actually work and why they're important. You've probably changed your own views and opinions while reading this book, so why not share your newfound knowledge with others? It's great for you to have implemented healthy communication in your own relationships, but it becomes so much more effective when all participants in the relationship are actively engaged in bettering themselves and gaining self-awareness of their limitations.

Educating Others on the Importance of Boundaries

Educating others doesn't have to mean standing in front of a room and giving a lecture. You can start small by introducing them to the immediate people in your life. The more you educate those around you about boundaries, the better the relationships and interactions you have can become.

Here are some tips for putting this into practice:

- Lead by example. The best way to show people how effective boundaries can be is to use them in your own life and let them see the results.
- Facilitate open discussions about boundaries, what they mean, and how they can benefit people in all aspects of their lives.
- Make them practical by giving people real-life examples of how boundaries can work and explaining how they can be implemented.
- Avoid giving targeted advice on where someone needs boundaries in their life because they might get offended or feel attacked.

Becoming a Boundary Advocate in Your Community

Once you feel confident in your ability to educate others on boundaries, you might feel inclined to start advocating for them in your local community. Being proactive in teaching others about being more assertive about their wants and needs is a great way for you to continue learning and growing on your journey in setting boundaries. The more you teach, the more you'll learn.

Here are some ideas of how you can begin advocating within your local community:

- Host workshops where you educate community members about boundaries and do activities with them to show them how to create their own.
- Get in touch with local organizations, schools, and churches that will allow you to give talks on and raise awareness about boundaries.
- Create pamphlets and leaflets outlining the importance and benefits of boundaries that you can hand out to people you meet.
- Reach out to local businesses about incorporating workshops about professional boundaries into their employee-training programs.
- Contact local schools and youth centers and see if they'd be willing to include boundaries in their curriculum or invite you to give students talks about them.

Being the first to do something is never easy, and it's not something that many people feel they can do. However, if you're able to share your knowledge and benefit the broader community within which you live, you should grab that opportunity with both hands.

Conclusion

Having personal boundaries is a great first step but being able to live in a society where the people around you also respect them will improve your quality of life exponentially. There isn't anybody in this world who wouldn't benefit from learning how to set and implement personal boundaries. Many people don't even realize how much they need them or how much having them will transform their lives.

In the next chapter, we'll be reflecting on how boundary setting is more than just a tool for implementing changes in your relationships but how they are a guide toward personal transformation. We'll also be looking at boundaries more holistically and discussing how you can use these newfound skills going forward into the future.

10. Reflections and Moving Forward

Make good boundaries your goal. They are your right, your responsibility, your greatest source of dignity.

— Elaine N. Aron

I have seen the power of boundaries not just in my life but in the lives of those around me. I have undergone such an intense period of transformation since I began this journey, and it's had a widespread impact on every area of my life. I used to be so unsure of myself, so apologetic, as if I was sorry for taking up space in this world. Now, I am empowered to claim my own space and be my own person.

As an immigrant, the urge to conform for the sake of fitting into a new culture nearly cost me my identity. But, through determining my boundaries, I have learned that, not only does my rich cultural heritage make up a big part of who I am, but it also makes me an invaluable asset in professional and social discussions where I'm able to offer a new perspective and new ideas.

Through self-care, I have slowly begun to release the burden of expectations that have weighed down on me for my entire life. There are so many labels I carried that made me feel like the world was on my shoulders: I had been trying to be a good friend, a good daughter, a good role model to my younger siblings, a good wife, and a good employee. I had to shed all of these labels and the expectations that came along with them to get down to the core of who I was. Prioritizing self-care and gaining self-awareness has given me the power to do that. Now that I'm sure of myself and know what I want to be happy and what I need to succeed, I feel so much more whole.

At first, you might also have just thought of boundaries as the rules you make for yourself regarding your limits or the walls you put up between yourself and other people. I used to think that way, too. Now I know that these safeguards are like a compass that I can use to guide me in the right direction in life. My boundaries help me align my future with my values and beliefs, and they keep me from falling into situations that jeopardize my mental or emotional well-being. They also protect me from people who don't respect me or my needs.

In this chapter, we'll be reflecting on the transformative impact that boundaries have had on your journey thus far. Not just that—we'll also be looking to the future and how you can keep reaping the benefits going forward.

Personal Reflections on Setting Boundaries

Encouraging Self-Analysis and Continuous Improvement

Self-analysis is a tool you can use to recognize how your thoughts, actions, and behaviors are impacting your ability to set and maintain healthy boundaries. There are many benefits of this, for example:

- You become more aware of what boundaries you might still need.
- You're able to dissect your interactions to better understand and identify scenarios where your boundaries might have been violated, or even those where you feel you did a good job in standing your ground.
- You're also able to learn from your mistakes by identifying situations where you possibly could have responded differently or where you might need to adjust your boundaries.

To continually improve your boundary-setting skills, you need to be perpetually working to expand your knowledge and understanding of yourself and how you want to be treated and how boundaries apply to your life. You can do this by getting feedback from others, watching how the people around you go about setting and maintaining their boundaries and keeping abreast of the educational material available on the subject. If you want to keep growing, you need to keep learning.

Reflective Practices for Assessing Boundary Effectiveness

Regularly taking time to pause and reflect is one of the best ways to ensure your continued growth and development. When you sit down and reflect on your personal protection mechanisms, you're more easily able to assess their effectiveness and identify areas that might require some improvement. You allow yourself the space to make more informed choices regarding whether certain boundaries are working for you, and you can also observe your own behavior and see how you might not be properly or effectively communicating some of them.

Learning from Successes and Setbacks

There is something to be learned from both your successes and the setbacks you've experienced throughout your boundary-setting journey.

When you succeed, you can learn how to adapt those same strategies to other situations where improvement is necessary. You can take note of how you communicated your boundaries in those situations, and you can remember to try and use the same effective phrases and expressions in future interactions. You are able to glean the tangible benefits. You can see the improvements in your relationships, your work life, and your self-care practices.

On the other hand, you won't always get it right. As much as setbacks can be disappointing, there are still important lessons you can learn from them, and you can use that information to prevent yourself from repeating the same mistakes in the future. Often, when your boundaries are violated, you can look back on the situation and try to see if there were any red flags that you might have missed. If you're emotionally triggered, you can assess what led up to the situation and how you can protect yourself from being exposed to that trigger in the future.

The Broader Impact of Boundaries

After seeing the effects and impact of boundaries on yourself and then exploring them in your relationships, it's easier to see how having them in place can have great benefits for society in general. While yours may be about you, their impact is universal.

The Role of Boundaries in Shaping Societal Norms

Societal norms can be defined as the unspoken rules within a society or culture that dictate what kinds of attitudes, behaviors, and beliefs the people within it find acceptable. These norms are what constitute a sense of belonging within the group or community, and people tend to shy away from violating them, for fear of rejection or alienation. When society begins to respect personal boundaries, this can influence what becomes the norm, and it can have an impact on shared ideas of what is acceptable behavior.

The Influence of Effective Setting Boundaries on Future Generations

When we set healthy boundaries for our lives and within our relationships, it becomes a benchmark for our children's attitudes toward them. Many dysfunctional family patterns are passed down, but when we assert our boundaries, we're able to break this cycle of dysfunction and free ourselves and our children from repeating it.

By modeling healthy boundaries, we also set an example that our children can follow. When we demonstrate setting and maintaining healthy boundaries, we're imparting valuable skills to the next generation that they will carry with them for the rest of their lives.

Envisioning a World With Respectful and Healthy Boundaries

In a world where everyone respected each other's boundaries, life would be far more harmonious. Conflicts would be reduced to meaningful discussions of our differences, and nobody would feel used or mistreated. People would feel safe to express their needs and wants and know that they will be respected by others.

We would all be able to embrace diversity and show empathy and compassion when dealing with people from different cultural backgrounds. We'd be more willing to learn and less likely to judge people who had values and beliefs that differed from ours.

We'd all feel empowered and able to care for our emotional and physical needs before taking care of others. We would give only as much as we were willing and capable of without others expecting us to give more.

Embracing the Future of Boundaries

The skill of setting boundaries is always changing and evolving. The tools that serve you now may no longer be effective in a few years' time. You need to continually work on them, learning from your mistakes and gaining encouragement from your successes.

Preparing for New Challenges and Opportunities

As much as you can learn and read about how to set boundaries in different and even difficult contexts, the reality is that you may still face challenges you hadn't anticipated. By building yourself a strong set of tools for standing your ground, you'll have the confidence to go into these situations without experiencing self-doubt. You can see unexpected situations as opportunities to learn new ways of doing things and new strategies for effectively and assertively communicating and implementing your boundaries.

Continuing the Journey of Personal Growth and Boundary Mastery

Boundary setting is something you will need and use for the rest of your life. It's not one of those things you learn once and never need to gain more knowledge on again, like riding a bike. As the world changes and grows and as you transition through various stages of life, so must you continue to develop your boundary-setting skills.

Through putting into practice the skills and strategies we've explored this far, you will be able to draw on a solid foundation of knowledge in the practice of establishing and maintaining boundaries. Use this as the springboard to catapult yourself further in your personal goals and aspirations.

Conclusion

Just as soon as our journey began, so it has come to an end. Although this concludes our path together, I sincerely hope it's only the beginning of your road with boundaries. May the knowledge you've gained within these pages form the foundation of your new life.

Thank you for sharing this experience with me, I hope the stories I've shared with you from my journey have inspired you to start setting more boundaries in your own life.

The path toward developing effective boundaries and honing your skills is not a smooth one. In fact, you could even imagine it as a maze. There are endless twists and turns, and you might not always choose the right direction. When you come to a dead end or realize that the course you're on doesn't lead to where you need to be, don't get disheartened or give up. Just backtrack and try again. The best part of learning is the road you take to where you want to be. So, don't give up.

Remember that boundaries are not selfish or rude. They are a way for you to protect yourself from feeling mistreated and taken advantage of. They are the lines you get to draw for yourself to stop you from giving too much of yourself away. Your needs and desires are just as important as those of others—never forget that.

Don't give away so much of your energy that you have none left for yourself. Prioritize self-care and don't neglect yourself in favor of helping those around you. When you set boundaries in your relationships, you help people understand how you'd like to be treated. When you reinforce those boundaries, you show them that you respect yourself, your time, and your energy. The best way for you to show people that boundaries matter is to implement them yourself.

You'll be surprised how even the smallest changes make the biggest difference so start small! You don't need to do a massive overhaul of all your relationships. Boundaries are a lifelong process and an endless journey, so there's no need to rush. The first step is to look inward. Get to know yourself, get to know what your values and beliefs are, and identify your limits and your triggers. When you're confident in who you are, it's so much easier to know what you need.

Having a clear understanding of what your needs are and why they matter will also make communicating them with others much simpler. Be prepared for people's reactions but also understand that their emotions are not your responsibility. You cannot control how other people think or act. You can only control your actions and decisions.

Sometimes setting boundaries can be difficult, and you might want to give up or let things slide, but I urge you not to do this. Consistency is the only way to ensure your limits are respected both by yourself and others. But that doesn't mean enforcing them without mercy.

Ethical boundary setting will help you learn how to assert yourself and communicate in a way that doesn't cause harm to others. It will remind you that, even though you have a right to protect yourself, so does everyone else! Use compassion to fuel yourself along the journey of establishing your boundaries. Appreciate that other people also have needs and that, through mutual respect and a little compromise, you can find a way to make sure that everyone's needs are met and that everyone feels safe and comfortable.

And, once you've gotten to a place where you feel confident in your boundaries, share the love. Educate others about the importance of having them and advocate for everyone's right to implement them. Create safe spaces where people can explore what it means to establish their limits without the influences of community norms or cultural pressures. Be sensitive to the fact that we live in a diverse world and not everyone shares the same values you do. Learn how to establish boundaries in an inclusive way that respects other people's customs and values.

Boundaries are about so much more than making your needs and desires a priority. They teach people how to treat you, and they allow you to learn how others would like to be treated in return. They help you create a world where everyone is respected and made to feel safe. A world where everyone is validated and not living under the constant pressure to do more than they're capable of or give more than they're willing to. Boundaries are about accepting your limitations and realizing that it's okay to say no sometimes.

Boundaries have taught me so many things about myself, my loved ones, and the world around me that I never would have learned otherwise. Yes, I have lost relationships, but I have gained so much more. The people I have in my life now validate my needs and enhance my experiences. I no longer find myself in situations where I feel used or manipulated. I have found a balance between my work and personal life that works for me, and I have found fulfillment in my interactions with people from all walks of life. Boundaries have done all of that for me and, if you let them, I have no doubt that they will do it for you, too.

Keeping the Game Alive

Congratulations on completing your journey through **Balanced Boundaries**!

Now that you're equipped with the tools to create healthier relationships and live a more balanced life, it's time to share your newfound wisdom with others.

By leaving your honest review on Amazon, you're not just expressing your thoughts; you're guiding other readers toward the same transformation you've experienced. Your review can help others discover the path to better boundaries and personal growth.

Thank you for your support. The message of **Balanced Boundaries** thrives when we share our insights – and your review is a crucial part of keeping this conversation alive.

Your feedback not only helps future readers, but it also supports me in my mission to spread the principles of balanced living. Together, we can make a positive impact on countless lives.

- With gratitude, S.H. Rhodes

Bonus Chapter: 21-Day Balanced Boundaries Challenge

Purpose of the Challenge

Thank you again for completing the book with me. I hope you have gained some valuable knowledge that you can implement in your life. Let's do a little practice together, day by day, for 21 days. This is a chance to focus on one practice at a time, to learn and strengthen boundary-setting skills. The goal is to foster personal growth and enhance life balance.

For the next 21 days, I would like you to focus on one task a day. That's what you should concentrate on. Make sure you have enough time to think, and gradually, you will acquire all the skills you need. Please do not stop after our 21-day challenge. Our vision is to find empowerment and take control back in our lives. This should continue as you go in every stage of your life.

Good luck! And let's do it together!

Day 1: Self-assessment day

Today, we are going to do a little assessment. Reflect on your boundaries in all of your current relationships. What are your closest relationships, and what do you feel you need to improve the most? Don't just think; it's a good idea to take a pen and paper or even type on your computer. Write down your current problems, and you can easily decide what you should do next. For example, you might spend too much time with a friend, or you and your significant other often do things that take too much of your time. Or one of your friends might be clearly taking advantage of you. Or you feel you are saying yes to people too often and are worried that you will offend them if you say no. Today's task is to reflect on your current boundaries and journal about areas needing improvement.

- Reflect on your current boundaries.
- Journal about areas you feel need improvement.

Day 2: Define your boundaries

Today, we are going to try to draw the boundaries for the problems you wrote down yesterday. Think about "what if." What would you do to change the situation and start making you feel you are controlling your life? Write down what you think you need to work on. Today's task is to write down specific boundaries you wish to set in your personal and professional life.

- Write down specific boundaries you wish to set in your personal and professional life.

Day 3: Communicate a boundary to a close one

Today, we are going to try to implement a boundary by starting to learn to communicate with a close one whom you are very comfortable talking about things. Tell them what you are looking to change in order to start taking control of your life back, and you would like this person to support and help you. By doing this, you are learning to open up and communicate your needs, and this might feel uncomfortable, but starting with someone close to you will help in practicing this uncomfortableness. Stepping out for the first step is the most important part. Eventually, you will overcome the awkwardness, and it will fade away, and you will be very open to talking to an acquaintance about your needs and how you'd like to be treated.

Today's task is to practice speaking out.

- Practice expressing a boundary to a friend or family member.

Day 4: Workplace or school boundary

Do you often do something you are not supposed to during your working/school hours, such as chit-chatting with others when you should be focused? Or talking about work during lunch break? Playing on your phone when you should be working? Yes, it's nice to scroll through videos sometimes, and that could make you relax, but do you know once you shift your focus to something else, you need to spend 15 minutes to get your full focus back? This is proven by the experiment. The time that you spend switching on and off can take so much more time than you need. Try to focus on one thing when you are doing it. It could be hard at first, but this can benefit your life because it could save you a lot of time, and eventually, you can have more time to relax at the end! For example, you might be working on something on and off for 5 hours to complete a project; but if you put your full focus on it, for 30 minutes to an hour or more if you can, then take a break for 15 minutes, then go back to it and repeat the method, you might only need to spend 3 hours to complete your project!

Today's task is to focus on what you need to work on to focus more. Let's start with that.

- Set a boundary at work, like a lunch break without work talk.

Day 5: Digital detox start

Do you know that you can check your average screen time usage in your phone? Check it now and see how long it is in a week, and per day average. In a recent research, Americans spend an average of almost 7 hours on the phone daily. If you are more than this number, you might need to consider managing your time more efficiently! If you are less than this number, that's good! But still try to get it down to less than 2-3 hours. But this also depends on the content you are accessing. If you are only watching videos that are not really helpful for your life, and you often don't know what you have done and the time has passed, if you ask yourself what you did in the last few hours and you cannot explain, then this is a big sign that you are just wasting your time. Today's task is to try to reduce the screen time. We don't have to start big, just reduce your normal screen time. For example, if you like to scroll your phone for 30 minutes in the morning, we don't need to change it to another habit right away, but we can try to reduce it to 15 minutes. Maybe you like to scroll your phone before bedtime for 1 hour, let's try 30 minutes, etc.

The time that you save, you could use it to spend some quality time for yourself and your family.

Today's task is to start small! When you start scrolling the phone, look at the time that you started, then again keep looking at the time, force yourself to close the app when 15 minutes are up.

- Initiate a period of reduced digital device usage.

Day 6: Personal space day

Today is a day for yourself. Do things you can, spend some time alone. Maybe go watch a movie in a movie theater, or go to a restaurant by yourself. Do one thing that you normally won't do if you are by yourself. Today's task is to challenge yourself to do something without a partner.

Let's do it! Conquer the uneasiness, and you will realize that it is not difficult and you might be getting to like it!

- Spend time alone, respecting your own boundaries.

Day 7: Reflection day

We are going to do some reflection today on how your week has gone so far! Did you follow all the steps for each day without skipping any of them? We will keep implementing what we have learned from the first week into our second week. We will add more as we go.

- Reflect on the first week and journal the experiences and feelings you encountered.

Day 8: No overcommitment

Let's try to learn to say no. Today, say no to something that is not on your plan. You will actually feel great afterward because you stood up for yourself, and you earned yourself more time, and most importantly, you had the courage to say it when you needed to. Write down what you decline at the end of the day!

- Say no to an extra task or commitment.

Day 9: Set a health boundary

The goal of setting boundaries is to achieve your personal well-being. This means a healthy lifestyle. It can be a workout routine; if you don't have the motivation to do it yourself, sign up for a weekly class that you must force yourself to go to, and that's only once a week. Or you could start a healthy diet one day in a week. No junk food, sugar, or fast food that day. Remember, you don't have to make a big change right away, let's start small, for example, just once a week. Then gradually, you can do 2 days in a week, or eventually 3-4 days a week.

- Implement a health-related boundary, like a workout routine or diet change.

Day 10: Emotional boundary exercise

We all like to hear stories sometimes. We often fall into gossip hours during work or in school. We have friends that we go to when we feel upset or when they need us. That's what friends are for, right? But today, we are learning not to take on their emotional baggage. It can become too much and drain our own energy when we hear it too often. When this happens to me, I tell my coworker, "Hey, I really need some good energy today. I am sorry you are feeling down, but I can't take this negativity." And encourage them to say and think positive things. Because of the laws of attraction. You keep thinking of something negative, it will only go that way. I truly believe this rule, because it works for me, and it's not only a belief. So this is your work today. If someone comes to you with low energy, you know what you should do.

- Practice not taking on someone else's emotional baggage.

Day 11: Revisit digital boundaries

Today, let's take a moment to reassess your digital detox plan. How has it been going? Are there areas where you could improve or adjust? Maybe you've noticed certain times of day are harder to stick to the plan, or perhaps there's a specific app that's particularly tempting. Whatever it is, take some time to tweak your digital boundaries to better suit your needs. Again, this is hard at first, but it will become a habit! The key is to be persistent and remind yourself of the benefits you're gaining from this practice.

- Assess and adjust your digital detox plan.

Day 12: Boundary reinforcement

Boundaries are meant to be respected, but sometimes they are challenged. Today, focus on reasserting a boundary that someone has been pushing against. It could be something like saying no to an extra task at work, additional favors from your family and friends, or something more significant, like standing up for your personal space. If you have a kid, it's a great opportunity for leading by action. They watch and learn to understand what a healthy boundary is. This is to show them they need to stand strong for their personal space.

You will be helping them to craft a successful life. Remember, maintaining boundaries is an ongoing process. It's not just about setting them once and forgetting about them; it's about consistently upholding them, even when it's challenging.

- Reassert a boundary that's being challenged.

Day 13: Seek support

Setting boundaries can be tough, and it's okay to seek support. Today, have a chat with a supportive friend, family member, or therapist about your journey in setting boundaries. Share your successes, your challenges, and anything you've learned along the way. This is a great opportunity to gain some perspective and encouragement. If your family and friends want you to be happy, they will be supportive and offer you some good advice as an outsider. Remember, it's important to surround yourself with people who respect your boundaries and support your growth.

- Discuss your boundary-setting journey with a supportive person.

Day 14: Mid-challenge reflection

We're halfway through the challenge! Take some time today to journal about your progress. What have you learned about yourself? What challenges have you faced, and how have you overcome them? What are the fears you have? Reflecting on your journey can provide valuable insights and motivation to continue. Consider how the boundaries you've set are impacting your life and relationships. Are there any adjustments you need to make going forward? This reflection will help you stay focused and committed to your boundary-setting goals. If they are not going in the direction you are hoping for, revise them.

- Journal about your progress and the challenges you've faced so far.

Day 15: Mindfulness practice

Mindfulness is a powerful tool in understanding and respecting your boundaries. Today, we are going to try a mindfulness activity, such as meditation, deep breathing, or a mindful walk with or without music. Focus on your personal needs and feelings, and how they relate to your boundaries. Pay attention to any thoughts or emotions that arise during this practice, and consider how they might inform your approach to setting and maintaining boundaries. This mindfulness exercise can help you stay centered and connected to your true self as you navigate your boundary-setting journey.

- Engage in a mindfulness activity, focusing on your personal needs and feelings.

Day 16: Declutter day

A cluttered space can often reflect a cluttered mind. Today, organize a physical space in your home, workspace, or even your car. Setting a boundary about your environment can help you feel more in control and at peace. Plus, a tidy space is just plain nice to be in! Take this opportunity to let go of things that no longer serve you or fit within your boundaries. As you declutter, consider how the physical act of organizing can mirror the process of setting and maintaining boundaries in other areas of your life.

- Organize a physical space, setting a boundary about your environment.

Day 17: Financial boundary

Money can be a tricky area to navigate. Today, set a financial boundary, like a budget limit for the week or a spending freeze on non-essential items. I used to be a big Amazon shopper; I bought a lot of things that seemed useful on the surface but weren't actually useful for me personally or my household. Are you also a person who adds a bunch of items to the cart and eventually deletes them? Do you realize how much time you waste creating a list only to delete it later?

We all have a craving for shopping. We might fall into the trap of buying a few items that aren't really necessary and spending money that could be better used elsewhere. Are you able to resist accessing the shopping app unless you genuinely need something? If not, let's try to reduce and cross out a few items at a time. Being mindful of your finances is an important aspect of self-care.

Reflect on your spending habits and identify areas where you can cut back without sacrificing your quality of life.

- Set a financial boundary, like a budget limit.

Day 18: Social media boundary

Social media can be a major time-sink and can sometimes negatively affect our mental health. As we mentioned in the book, who you follow can have a huge impact on your mental well-being. Do you think the people you follow make you feel less about yourself, or do you feel motivated and comfortable? Today, let's go through the list of people you follow and unfollow those who are not helpful for your life. And be careful not to accidentally fall into reading their profiles and spending hours on it! You should have a strong mindset that this is what you're going to do today. But that doesn't mean you should spend all day doing it. Limit your social media usage to a specific time of day or set a time limit for how long you'll spend on it. This exercise is also a practice in self-control and discipline.

- Limit your social media usage to a specific time of the day.

Day 19: Assertive communication practice

Assertiveness is key in setting and maintaining boundaries. Today, practice assertive communication in any scenario. It could be something as simple as requesting a correction on your coffee order, or as complex as addressing a recurring issue with a coworker. Start with your daily life, whether it's with your household family, your neighbor, or even someone you walk past on the street. If you don't feel confident, you can start by pretending; that's what I did, and it will eventually become part of your personality! You are not faking, you are just practicing it.

- Practice assertive communication in a challenging scenario.

Day 20: Preparing to maintain boundaries

As we near the end of the challenge, it's time to think about how you'll sustain your boundaries. Today, make a plan for maintaining the boundaries you've set during this challenge. What strategies have worked well for you? How will you continue to enforce your boundaries? Our goal is to improve our lives and take control back; this is a marathon, not something you can change drastically right away. If you face a challenge, find another way. Remember that it's like you are walking in a maze, just like the book cover; the person at the entrance is you. You still have a long journey to go! But what makes the most fun is the process. Reflect on your journey so far and set intentions for how you will continue to prioritize and respect your boundaries in the future.

- Make a plan for how you will sustain your boundaries post-challenge.

Day 21: Celebration and reflection

Congratulations, you've completed the 21-Day Boundary Setting Challenge! Today, take some time to celebrate your accomplishment. Reflect on the journey you've been on, the growth you've experienced, and how you'll carry these lessons forward. Remember, setting and maintaining boundaries is an ongoing process, and you've taken a big step in the right direction. Let's write down your appreciation for yourself for what you have done so far and encouragement for the future you, if you face difficulties. I hope to see you on the other side after you complete the maze!

- Celebrate the completion of the challenge.

References

Alison. (2023, May 22). *Challenges to self-care (Let's overcome the obstacles)* Alison's Notebook. https://alisonsnotebook.com/challenges-to-self-care/

Aslam, A., Eugster, J., Ho, G., Jaumotte, F., & Piazza, R. (2018, April 9). *Globalization helps spread Knowledge and technology across borders.* International Monetary Fund. https://www.imf.org/en/Blogs/Articles/2018/04/09/globalization-helps-spread-knowledge-and-technology-across-borders

Associates, N. (2023, July 25). *Managers: 5 essential reasons why values-based boundaries are important.* LinkedIn. https://www.linkedin.com/pulse/managers-5-essential-reasons-why-values-based-boundaries#:

Bay Area CBT Center. (2023, November 21). *How to develop interdependence in relationships.* https://bayareacbtcenter.com/how-to-develop-interdependence-in-relationships/

Bev. (2023, February 8). *The barriers to setting boundaries.* The Women's Vault. https://www.thewomensvault.com/setting-boundaries-barriers/

Blaschka, A. (2022, April 9). *The 2 seemingly opposite traits that work together to drive your career.* Forbes. https://www.forbes.com/sites/amyblaschka/2022/04/09/the-2-seemingly-opposite-traits-that-work-together-to-drive-your-career/?sh=7b3062b95951

Boynton, E. (2021, May 17). *How to set and maintain boundaries.* Right as Rain. https://rightasrain.uwmedicine.org/mind/mental-health/boundaries#:

Bradley, J. (2023, July 6). *The role of boundaries in personal growth and transformation.* Medium. https://johnbradley1.medium.com/the-role-of-boundaries-in-personal-growth-and-transformation-50032213c4fe

Brady, S. (2021, October 11). *The sensitivity of boundary setting in collectivist cultures.* Counseling Today. https://ct.counseling.org/2021/10/the-sensitivity-of-boundary-setting-in-collectivist-cultures/

Burton, T. N. (2023, January 17). *Get over your fear of setting boundaries.* Medium. https://medium.com/@mstashab/get-over-your-fear-of-setting-boundaries-b93bb8c73c6f

Carter, B. (2023a, May 1). *Building resilience through boundaries: How to*

bounce back from life's challenges. The Daily Positive. https://www.thedai
lypositive.com/boundaries-and-resilience/

Carter, B. (2023b, May 1). *How setting boundaries helps cultivate a growth mindset.* The Daily Positive. https://www.thedailypositive.com/bound
aries-and-growth-mindset/#:

Clarke, J. (2023, February 13). *Interdependence can Build a lasting and safe relationship.* Verywell Mind. https://www.verywellmind.com/how-to-
build-a-relationship-based-on-interdependence-4161249#toc-how-to-
build-an-interdependent-relationship

Dodson, J. (n.d.). *How to set boundaries with friends—and when to do it.* BetterHelp. https://www.betterhelp.com/advice/general/how-to-set-
boundaries-with-friends-and-when-to-do-it/

Etessam, S. (2023, April 10). *Council post: The real challenges of boundaries at work.* Forbes. https://www.forbes.com/sites/forbescommunication
scouncil/2023/04/10/the-real-challenges-of-boundaries-at-work/?sh=
103963611200

Field, B. (2023, July 13). *How to set boundaries with friends—and why it's neces-sary.* Verywell Mind. https://www.verywellmind.com/how-to-set-
boundaries-with-friends-7503205#toc-supporting-friendship-and-its-
boundaries

Geriach, J. (2024, March 7). *4 keys to setting effective boundaries.* Psychology Today. https://www.psychologytoday.com/za/blog/beyond-mental-
health/202403/4-secrets-to-setting-effective-boundaries

Gilies, G. (2024, March 6). *The importance of boundaries in romantic relation-ships— Relationship problems? EUR" tools to build and maintain a healthy marriage.* Www.mentalhelp.net. https://www.mentalhelp.net/blogs/the-
importance-of-boundaries-in-romantic-relationships/

Goss, R. (2019, November 20). *3 steps for how to communicate boundaries in relationships.* INLP Center. https://inlpcenter.org/how-to-communi
cate-boundaries-in-relationships/

Hailey, L. (n.d.). *How to set boundaries: 5 ways to draw the line politely.* Science of People. https://www.scienceofpeople.com/how-to-set-boundaries/

Haupt, A. (2023, October 18). *6 ways to set boundaries at work.* TIME. https://
time.com/6323105/how-to-set-boundaries-at-work/

Heverly, C. (2015, August 19). *Things to consider when posting online—Part 1: Boundaries.* MSU Extension. https://www.canr.msu.edu/news/
things_to_consider_when_posting_online_part_1_boundaries

Holly. (2019, April 8). *Overcoming the top 3 challenges to self-care.* The

Commons.   https://commonslibrary.org/overcoming-the-top-3-chal
lenges-to-self-care/

Horn, H. V. (2023, February 23). *Boundaries are still vital in a long-distance
relationship. Here's how to set them.* The List. https://www.thelist.com/
1209113/boundaries-are-still-vital-in-a-long-distance-relationship-
heres-how-to-set-them/

Indeed Editorial Team. (2022, August 8). *6 steps to discover your core values.*
Indeed Career Guide. https://www.indeed.com/career-advice/career-
development/discover-core-values

Indeed Editorial Team. (2023, August 31). *16 ways to set healthy boundaries at
work.* Indeed Career Guide. https://www.indeed.com/career-advice/
career-development/boundaries-at-work

Juby, B. (2016, May 17). *Personal boundaries: Types and how to set them.* Psych
Central.   https://psychcentral.com/relationships/what-are-personal-
boundaries-how-do-i-get-some#how-to-set-boundaries

Juby, B. (2022, October 28). *Signs your boundaries are being violated: Examples
and how to deal.* Psych Central. https://psychcentral.com/relationships/
signs-boundary-violations#pressures

Khoddam, R. (2023, December 29). *8 ways to cope with life transitions.*
Psychology Today. https://www.psychologytoday.com/us/blog/the-
addiction-connection/202312/8-ways-to-cope-with-life-transitions

Koehler, J. (2023, May 16). *10 core values to guide behavior.* Psychology
Today. https://www.psychologytoday.com/intl/blog/beyond-school-
walls/202305/10-core-values-to-guide-behavior

Kuhl, A. (2022, April 11). *The importance of personal and professional boundaries in everyday life.* Mindful Keeping. https://www.mindfulkeeping.
com.au/the-importance-of-personal-and-professional-boundaries-in-
everyday-life/

LeClair, C. (2023, February 5). *Communicating boundaries.* LinkedIn. https://
www.linkedin.com/pulse/communicating-boundaries-cassandra-
leclair-ph-d-#:~:text=Practice%20self%2Dcare%20and%20take

Legg, T. J. (2018, December 10). *The No BS Guide to Setting Healthy
Boundaries in Real Life.* Healthline. https://www.healthline.com/health/
mental-health/set-boundaries#learn-other-peoples-boundaries-too

Leonard, E. (2021, August 14). *Boundary anxiety and fear is real.* Psychology
Today.   https://www.psychologytoday.com/us/blog/peaceful-parent
ing/202108/boundary-anxiety-and-fear-is-real

Lunkka, N., Jansson, N., Mainela, T., Suhonen, M., Meriläinen, M., Puhakka,

V., & Wiik, H. (2021). Professional boundaries in action: Using reflective spaces for boundary work to incorporate a new healthcare role. *Human Relations, 75*(7), 1270. https://www.academia.edu/76084980/ Professional_boundaries_in_action_Using_reflective_spaces_ for_boundary_work_to_incorporate_a_new_healthcare_role

Margolies, L. (2019, November 16). *How to set boundaries with difficult people: Do's and don'ts.* Psych Central. https://psychcentral.com/lib/how-to-set-boundaries-with-difficult-people#Examples-of-effective-and-ineffective-limit-setting:

Martin, S. (2016, July 11). *How to deal with people who repeatedly violate your boundaries.* Psych Central. https://psychcentral.com/blog/imperfect/ 2016/07/how-to-deal-with-people-who-repeatedly-violate-your-boundaries#Now

Martin, S. (2018, April 24). *What are boundaries and why do I need them?* Live Well With Sharon Martin. https://www.livewellwithsharonmartin. com/what-are-boundaries/

Martin, S. (2020, April 23). *7 types of boundaries you may need.* Psych Central. https://psychcentral.com/blog/imperfect/2020/04/7-types-of-boundaries-you-may-need#6)-Time-Boundaries

Martin, S. (2021, April 17). *7 Types of Boundaries You Need to Set.* The Better Boundaries Workbook. https://betterboundariesworkbook.com/types-of-boundaries/

Meagan. (2021, March 6). *7 self-care boundaries (to finally start putting yourself first).* Okay Now Breathe. https://www.okaynowbreathe.com/self-care-boundaries/

MedCircle. (2020, October 13). *How to set boundaries with family: The definitive guide.* MedCircle. https://medcircle.com/articles/how-to-set-boundaries-with-family/

Miller, L. (2023). Supervision to support reflective practices. *Journal of Educational Supervision, 6*(1), 1–18. https://doi.org/10.31045/jes.6.1.1

Molitor, M. (2024, January 1). *Embracing boundaries: A journey of growth and self-discovery.* Construction2style.com. https://construction2style.com/ embracing-boundaries-a-journey-of-growth-and-self-discovery/

Nicole, A. (2019, August 22). *3 kind, simple & effective ways to communicate your boundaries.* Medium. https://headway.ginger.io/3-kind-simple-effective-ways-to-communicate-your-boundaries-46dad0989e79

Nollan, J. (2020, September 21). *How to deal with someone who repeatedly disrespects your boundaries.* A Conscious Rethink. https://www.acon

sciousrethink.com/14203/how-to-deal-with-someone-who-doesnt-respect-your-boundaries/

Ofoegbu, C. (2023, September 14). *Mastering the art of setting boundaries: A key to personal and professional success.* LinkedIn. https://www.linkedin.com/pulse/mastering-art-setting-boundaries-key-personal-success-ofoegbu-

Osborn, C. (2023, May 18). *How to set personal boundaries using tech to improve your well-being.* MUO. https://www.makeuseof.com/set-personal-boundariesn-tech-improve-well-being/

Park, R. (2021, March 18). *Understanding group dynamics—what every leader should know.* Roffey Park Institute. https://www.roffeypark.ac.uk/knowl edge-and-learning-resources-hub/understanding-group-dynamics-what-every-leader-should-know/

Pattemore, C. (2021, June 3). *10 ways to build and preserve better boundaries.* Psych Central. https://psychcentral.com/lib/10-way-to-build-and-preserve-better-boundaries

Pennington, D. A. (2020, December 26). *How to define your values + set clear boundaries.* Thrive Global. https://community.thriveglobal.com/how-to-define-your-values-set-clear-boundaries/

Perry, E. (2022, August 25). *How to set boundaries at work: A personal guide to drawing the line.* BetterUp. https://www.betterup.com/blog/how-to-set-boundaries-at-work

Piata, M. (2018, October 31). *How to spot your emotional triggers.* Psychology Today. https://www.psychologytoday.com/us/blog/the-gen-y-psy/201810/how-spot-your-emotional-triggers

Power of Positivity. (2019, June 15). *5 ways to respond to people who violate your boundaries.* https://www.powerofpositivity.com/5-ways-to-respond-to-people-who-violate-your-boundaries/#google_vignette

Power of Positivity. (2019, December 14). *5 ways to identify your emotional triggers (And how to handle them).* https://www.powerofpositivity.com/identify-emotional-triggers/

Priya, V. (2016, April 11). *Myths & misconceptions about boundaries.* Vicki Tidwell Palmer. https://vickitidwellpalmer.com/myths-misconceptions-boundaries/

Rabikrisson, A. (2023, August 22). *Council post: Effective ways to build and maintain personal and professional boundaries.* Forbes. https://www.forbes.com/sites/forbescoachescouncil/2023/08/22/effective-ways-to-build-and-maintain-personal-and-professional-boundaries/?sh=324864328f10

Rabinovich, M. (2023, June 19). *The power of boundaries: Nurturing harmonious relationships.* Mindfulness Therapy Services. https://mindfulness therapyservices.ca/the-power-of-boundaries-nurturing-harmonious-relationships/

Ratson, M. (2024, January 11). *Managing conflict resolution effectively.* Psychology Today. https://www.psychologytoday.com/us/blog/the-wisdom-of-anger/202401/managing-conflict-resolution-effectively

Rebecca. (2023, May 13). *10 ways to firmly set boundaries with family.* Minimalism Made Simple. https://www.minimalismmadesimple.com/home/boundaries-with-family/

Reed, C. (2023a, January 5). *Reevaluating your boundaries: When to adjust and stand firm.* The Daily Positive. https://www.thedailypositive.com/reeval uating-boundaries/

Reed, C. (2023b, May 1). *Self-reflection and boundaries: Understanding your personal limits.* The Daily Positive. https://www.thedailypositive.com/boundaries-and-self-reflection/

Reid, S. (2023, March 1). *Setting healthy boundaries in relationships.* Help Guide. https://www.helpguide.org/articles/relationships-communica tion/setting-healthy-boundaries-in-relationships.htm

Retta, M. (2019, November 22). *The importance of creating boundaries online in the digital age.* Yahoo Life. https://www.yahoo.com/lifestyle/impor tance-creating-boundaries-online-digital-170059804.html

Ross, M. (2023a, May 1). *Communicating your boundaries: How to be assertive and clear.* The Daily Positive. https://www.thedailypositive.com/commu nicating-your-boundaries/

Ross, M. (2023b, May 1). *Embracing cultural boundaries: Understanding and respecting diversity.* The Daily Positive. https://www.thedailypositive. com/cultural-boundaries/

Rusnak, K. (2021, June 11). *Setting boundaries efficiently.* Psychology Today. https://www.psychologytoday.com/us/blog/happy-healthy-relation ships/202106/setting-boundaries-efficiently

Scharff, C. (2022, February 6). *Six tips for setting strong personal boundaries.* Psychology Today. https://www.psychologytoday.com/us/blog/ending-addiction-for-good/202202/six-tips-for-setting-strong-personal-boundaries

Sheltering Wings. (n.d.). *Boundaries & expectations.* https://shelteringwings. org/prevent-abuse/40-developmental-assets/boundaries-expectations/

Schunk, S. (2014). *Professional boundaries: Common dilemmas and a framework for decision-making.* https://www.pcaaz.org/wp-content/uploads/

2014/07/D56-Managing-Common-Boundary-Dilemmas.pdf

Setting. (2020, April 22). *Setting digital boundaries: How to disconnect from work*. Staples. https://www.staples.com/content-hub/culture/health-wellness/setting-digital-boundaries-6-tips-on-how-to-disconnect-after-the-workday

Shafir, H. (2021, July 16). *How to set boundaries with friends (if you're too nice)*. SocialSelf. https://socialself.com/blog/boundaries-friends/

Shandilya, P. (2023, April 30). *5 ways to balance independence and togetherness in a relationship*. Medium. https://priyansh-shandilya.medium.com/5-ways-to-balance-independence-and-togetherness-in-a-relationship-d003a6afc71a

Smith, J. (2024, January 8). *Embracing unconventional relationships in modern times*. Tech Me How. https://www.techmehow.com/embracing-unconventional-relationships-in-modern-times/

Strauss Cohen, I. (2017). *When guilt keeps you from setting boundaries*. Psychology Today. https://www.psychologytoday.com/us/blog/your-emotional-meter/201705/when-guilt-keeps-you-setting-boundaries

Tanner, A. (n.d.). *The vital role of boundaries in personal and professional life for maintaining mental health*. AlbertaTanner Coaching. https://albertatanner.com/blog/healthyboundaries

Tartakovsky, M. (2016, May 17). *10 tips for setting boundaries online*. Psych Central. https://psychcentral.com/lib/10-tips-for-setting-boundaries-online#1

Tartakovsky, M. (2018, December 9). *How empathic people can set effective, loving boundaries*. Psych Central. https://psychcentral.com/blog/how-empathic-people-can-set-effective-loving-boundaries#4

Tiglao-Guss, E. (2020, June 23). *How to overcome obstacles to self-care*. Grit & Virtue. https://gritandvirtue.com/how-to-overcome-obstacles-to-self-care/

Touchstone Publishers (2023a, October 22). *15 proven strategies for setting boundaries with difficult people*. https://touchstonepublishers.com/15-proven-strategies-for-setting-boundaries-with-difficult-people/

Touchstone Publishers. (2023b, October 22). *Six powerful techniques for setting personal boundaries*. https://touchstonepublishers.com/six-powerful-techniques-for-setting-personal-boundaries/

Vigliotti, A. (2020, December 10). *3 biggest myths about boundaries*. Psychology Today. https://www.psychologytoday.com/us/blog/the-now/202012/3-biggest-myths-about-boundaries

Wangmo, P. (2019, September 22). *What does setting boundaries mean in different cultures?* Medium. https://peggywangmo.medium.com/what-does-setting-boundaries-mean-in-different-cultures-197e3412cce8

Whispers of the Heart. (2024, January 25). *Unraveling manipulation: Navigating ethical boundaries in personal professional, and societal.* Medium. https://medium.com/@themabelbridge/unraveling-manipulation-navigating-ethical-boundaries-in-personal-professional-and-societal-b7bb6c3f8c5a

Whitener, S. (2019, December 11). *Council post: How setting boundaries positively impacts your self-esteem.* Forbes. https://www.forbes.com/sites/forbescoachescouncil/2019/12/11/how-setting-boundaries-positively-impacts-your-self-esteem/?sh=2cb95be2339c

Willisey, P. S. (2021, May 24). *How to set healthy boundaries in close relationships.* Psychology Today. https://www.psychologytoday.com/intl/blog/packing-success/202105/how-set-healthy-boundaries-in-close-relationships

Wilson, J. (2022, November 23). *What to do if you feel guilty after setting boundaries.* HuffPost. https://www.huffpost.com/entry/setting-boundaries-without-guilt_l_637b8f09e4b0c5739622d69f#:

Wolff, J. (2021). How is technology changing the world, and how should the world change technology? *Global Perspectives, 2*(1). https://doi.org/10.1525/gp.2021.27353

Wright-Garcia, E. (2023, July 25). *Three common misconceptions about boundaries.* Two Chairs. https://www.twochairs.com/blog/three-common-misconceptions-about-boundaries

Yuhas, J. (2023, April 12). *Fearful to set boundaries? Here are three ways to overcome it.* Jan and Jillian. https://www.janandjillian.com/relationship/fearful-to-set-boundaries-here-are-three-ways-to-overcome-it#:

Yuko, E. (2024, January 12). *Setting healthy personal and emotional boundaries —and why it matters.* Real Simple. https://www.realsimple.com/health/mind-mood/emotional-health/how-to-set-boundaries#toc-how-to-establish-boundaries-for-yourself

About the Author

S.H Rhodes, an esteemed author and guiding light in the field of setting boundaries and self-development, brings a wealth of personal experience and insight to her writing. As the eldest child among her siblings and cousins, Rhodes was constantly under the weight of familial expectations, tasked with being a role model in all aspects of life. This backdrop of her upbringing significantly shaped her understanding of the vital necessity of setting personal boundaries.

Rhodes' journey as an immigrant, living and working in a foreign country, further deepened her insights into self-development. She intimately knows the challenges of adapting to a new society, where one often feels compelled to accept everything, lower personal standards, and strive to be the best, often at the cost of one's well-being. These experiences, marked by stages of self-compromise and burnout, have played a crucial role in shaping her deep understanding and effective practice in boundary-setting.

Her mission is to empower individuals to recognize their worth and establish boundaries that foster personal growth and mental health. Rhodes' approach is empathetic and relatable, making her books a valuable resource for anyone struggling with the pressures of modern life.

S.H Rhodes' passion for helping others find balance and peace within themselves is contagious. Her goal is to reach as many people as possible, spreading the message that setting boundaries is not just about saying no, but about saying yes to a healthier, more fulfilling life. Her work continues to inspire and guide individuals on their journey to personal empowerment and well-being.

Also by S.H. Rhodes

In the past year, Rhodes has faced the profound loss of several loved ones, prompting her to embark on a journey of emotional exploration and heal- ing. Through her writing, she aims to share her experiences and insights, offering support and solace to others navigating similar paths of grief and personal growth. Her heartfelt storytelling reflects her resilience and commitment to transforming pain into strength.

This book is a personal journal that shares the author's journey of healing after the loss of loved ones. Unlike lengthy books, it is concise and straightforward, with related quotes at the start of each chapter to inspire and provide context. The book is designed to be easy to understand and to the point, serving as a guide for readers on their own paths to healing. It offers insights into what to expect during the grieving process and how to use these experiences as strength to move forward.

Made in the USA
Middletown, DE
22 October 2024